"Helping people forgive is one of the most common challenges I face in my therapeutic work. However, there has been little in terms of guidance or a reliable model for forgiveness. The authors have resolved this disconnect with *The Forgive for Good Recovery Workbook*. This workbook provides us with a road map for forgiving, and I have personally and professionally benefitted from Lyndon Harris's work."

> —**Richard Jones, MA, MBA, LCAS, CCS, CEAP, SAP, c-EMDR,** executive vice president and executive director for Heritage CARES, a division of Heritage Health Solutions in Coppell, TX

"The authors have provided a succinct and excellent workbook on building one of life's most critical tools for successful living: *forgiveness.* Although directed toward those seeking or in recovery, the lessons provided are for every reader. The tools and techniques provided to change thinking and remove our mental roadblocks are masterful and easy to follow. This book is on my Christmas list to those I care about."

> —**W. Dennis Derr, EdD,** retired behavioral health executive/consultant, and author of *Building Personal Resiliency*

"This workbook offers practical, important support that works alongside the12-step program to support those of us who have gotten stuck in the wounds of our past and hit roadblocks in our recovery. Based in solid research coupled with the wisdom of their own lived experience, the authors make a case for forgiveness as a vital step toward recovery and offer an accessible route toward this life-saving work."

> —**Rev. Brian Ammons, PhD,** cofounder and spiritual director of The Porch Community

"Personal, vulnerable, and well-grounded in research, Luskin and Harris offer wry insights into the universal experiences of resentment, pain, healing, and hope. This practical guide will help anyone motivated to rewrite their story and move forward with the lightness only forgiveness brings."

> —**Jeff Gorter, MSW,** vice president of clinical crisis response with R3 Continuum, a nationwide provider of workplace trauma/disaster response behavioral health services

"I have admired Luskin's forgiveness work since he was a postdoc at Stanford Medicine with me two decades ago. The workbook makes forgiveness available to anyone struggling with an addiction, and explains why forgiveness is essential. This important work continues to deepen and ripen, and the workbook format makes an invaluable contribution to people in recovery."

> —**Kenneth R. Pelletier,** author *Sound Mind, Sound Body* and *Change Your Genes, Change Your Life*

"This workbook offers a powerful and positive alternative to hitting the bottle or doing drugs to cope with the inevitable disappointments, resentments, and defeats of life. Luskin and Harris provide a perfect blend of science, self-help exercises, and stories to illuminate the healing potential of forgiveness and how to unlock it. Struggling with substance use is a common, challenging experience, and there is wisdom in this book that can help you *Forgive for Good*."

> —**Loren Toussaint, PhD,** chair of the Templeton World Charity Foundationand the Discover Forgiveness Advisory Council, and president of the Forgiveness Foundation

"I am an orthopedic spine surgeon who developed severe mental and physical pain for over thirteen years. I was introduced to Luskin's book, *Forgive for Good,* by a patient a couple of years later. It changed my life. As I shared his perspective through his book, my patients began to heal more consistently—not just improve, but have their lives transformed and thrive. I have witnessed hundreds of people break free from chronic mental and physical pain, which are direct causes of addiction. The tipping point is ALWAYS first recognizing anger and learning strategies to deal with it. Deep healing happens as you move forward into the life you choose, but you must first 'let go.' This book provides excellent, practical ways of allowing healing to happen."

> —**David Hanscom, MD,** author of *Do You Really Need Spine Surgery?*

"I've had the privilege of hosting Fred Luskin as a speaker at the World Happiness Summit for many years. His insights have profoundly impacted my life and the lives of thousands of others, but the most transformative lesson he's taught me is that happiness requires certain conditions, and forgiveness is one of the most essential. This powerful workbook—though designed for individuals and families navigating the challenges of substance abuse and recovery—offers valuable, research-backed tools that can help anyone master the art of forgiveness. If you want to be happier, forgive. This practical book shows you how."

> —**Karen Guggenheim,** CEO and founder of WOHASU and the World Happiness Summit

"Having worked with forgiveness in dozens of countries and war-torn places for close to half a century, the power of forgiving to transform and heal relationships and lives never ceases to amaze me. One of the most common questions I have heard over the years is, 'But how do I actually forgive?' Here we finally have an actual step-by-step, nonsectarian workbook that is the first to bring together research-based strategies of forgiveness for use in the large arena of recovery. Even more importantly, these same tools and practices have proven to be successful in a wide range of unresolved grievances and life experiences. I will recommend *The Forgive for Good Recovery Workbook* to the dozens of independent Centers for Attitudinal Healing located on six continents."

—**Diane Cirincione Jampolsky, PhD,** founder of Attitudinal Healing International

"It is a pleasure to endorse *The Forgive for Good Recovery Workbook*. Frederic Luskin has worked with the Stanford women's basketball team for eight years, and has established strong and trustworthy relationships with all of our players and coaches. We always looked forward to each session because of the benefit it was for everyone. Once at the NCAA Championship, the most stressful time of the season, I asked our team, 'What would help you the most?' and the answer was 'Let's do a Zoom with Fred.' Luskin was the inspiration for our 2024 team shirt motto which said, 'Do your best and forgive the rest.'"

—**Tara Vanderveer,** Stanford women's basketball coach and three-time national champion

"*The Forgive for Good Recovery Workbook* is an excellent guide to the difficult art of forgiveness. Through clear and simple step-by-step guidance, the book shows us how to forgive both ourselves and others. It is based on decades of research from the Stanford Forgiveness Project. If you want to be healthier, this book will teach you to release your grievances and move on."

—**Rangan Chatterjee,** *Sunday Times* best-selling author, and host of the most-listened-to health podcast in Europe: *Feel Better Live More*

"*The Forgive for Good Recovery Workbook* is an invaluable guide for those in recovery, blending scientific and spiritual perspectives on forgiveness. Written by two forgiveness experts who approach the subject from a very different point of view, the workbook empowers individuals to release resentment, heal emotional wounds, and take responsibility for their reactions and attitudes. Readers will appreciate the stories and prompts that nudge them toward self-reflection that can lead to a new sense of personal freedom, health, and joy."

—**Kathy Eldon,** author, producer, and founder of the Creative Visions Foundation

The Forgive for Good Recovery Workbook

Overcome Addiction, Heal Your Past, and Find Peace in Sobriety

Frederic Luskin, PhD
Lyndon Harris

New Harbinger Publications, Inc.

Publisher's Note

NEW HARBINGER PUBLICATIONS is a registered trademark of New Harbinger Publications, Inc.

New Harbinger Publications is an employee-owned company.

Copyright © 2025 by Frederic Luskin and Lyndon Harris
New Harbinger Publications, Inc.
5720 Shattuck Avenue
Oakland, CA 94609
www.newharbinger.com

Cover design by Amy Daniel

Acquired by Ryan Buresh

Edited by Karen Schader

Library of Congress Cataloging-in-Publication Data on file

Printed in the United States of America

27   26   25

10   9   8   7   6   5   4   3   2   1   First Printing

Contents

Foreword V

Introduction 1

CHAPTER 1   Forgiveness: What and Why 7

CHAPTER 2   The Power of Forgiveness: An Evidence-Based Approach ... 17

CHAPTER 3   What Forgiveness Is and Is Not 25

CHAPTER 4   Grievances and Revenge Fantasies 45

CHAPTER 5   The Healing Balm of Gratitude 63

CHAPTER 6   Helpful Tools: Change the Channel and PERT ... 79

CHAPTER 7   The Tyranny of Unenforceable Rules 95

CHAPTER 8   Change the Story, Change Your Life 111

CHAPTER 9   Self-Forgiveness and New Beginnings 123

CHAPTER 10 Guided Practice: HEAL and Self-HEAL 147

Acknowledgments 161

References 163

Foreword

Dr. Luskin and I first met about thirty years ago as panelists addressing the subject of forgiveness—he from the scientific, secular perspective and me from the personal, spiritual Twelve-Step methodology. Afterward, we agreed that the dynamic of the process is the same, but the vocabulary is quite different.

Today, we cofacilitate workshops for the recovery community, using our combined knowledge and experience to bring understanding and relief to those willing to confront their suffering and take responsibility for their healing and their freedom.

Forgiveness is a process, not an event. Its first step is the decision to give up resentments. Forgiveness requires an open mind and an open heart—and in addition, the willingness to do some very challenging work of self-reflection and owning of personal responsibility for our attitudes and actions.

Although Dr. Luskin addresses the toxic nature of resentments in the world of addiction, he broadly addresses the topic of forgiveness for *every* human being. The negative energy of anger and blame creates a poisonous shadow, blocking each person from the light of serenity and, therefore, happiness.

This workbook helps readers identify negative emotions manifesting as anger, resentment, envy, jealousy, fear, dishonesty, blame, guilt, shame, and a myriad of other clouds that block us from our human happiness…the sunlight of life.

Bottom line, we are not victims. Of course, many of us have been actual victims of one type or another. But now we must accept the unfortunate history of *our* history and move on. Easier said than done. I do not mean to diminish the real harm done. But the truth is, that harm is not happening *now*. We need to acknowledge our hurt, accept the impact on us of our *past* reality, and decide how to adjust to our *current* reality.

Most of us need help from an experienced objective person so that we can distinguish fact from fiction, feelings from reality. We need a sounding board to enable us to look into a mirror and see the cold, hard truth. We are not necessarily responsible for any of the surrounding events, persons, or circumstances. We are 100 percent responsible—right now—for our attitude, reactions, and behavior with respect to all previous and current events, people, and circumstances.

This is a workbook—emphasis on *work*—for those who want to be free from any and all negative emotions—whether of short- or long-term duration. Is there any shadow in your life blocking you from the sunlight of positive energy? This process will set you free. The promised outcomes are health, happiness, joy, a developed sense of individual agency, experience of personal empowerment—and most of all: a life of *freedom*!

We can walk our path free of darkness, illuminated by the light of truth. We cannot change our history. Many times, we cannot change our current life circumstances. But we can take personal ownership of our current attitude and reactions; then take healthy and corrective actions about it all.

This work will change your personal feelings about now, which will change your actions, which will create a more positive today and joy-filled tomorrow. The dimmer switch goes up a notch at a time and the lights get brighter incrementally—soon, brilliant enough to allow us to walk in warm sunshine.

Perhaps you feel that you are a prisoner in the jail of family origin construction. When you discover there are no real, objective walls, ceiling, or floor—only the bars you are holding before your face and looking through—you realize that all you need to do is release your grip on these bars and let them fall to the ground.

The simple, but not easy, formula:

Be willing to have an open mind and heart, to set aside all prior and current knowledge, emotions, and experiences.

Examine all your beliefs and expectations—cultural, family, and personal.

Challenge all your attitudes, perspectives, and motives by looking at your actual actions, reactions, and behaviors.

Identify all your wants and needs as embedded in your unenforceable rules, unrealistic beliefs, unhealthy stories, unhelpful fantasies, and unfortunate shoulds.

Accept that we are *now* not victims. At best, we are accomplices; at worst, we are the perpetrators.

Embrace the idea that we each need to hold a desire to be free, be willing to take responsibility for our individual reactions and actions, own our mistakes, and take 100 percent responsibility for our life as it manifests today.

Ask yourself: How free do I want to be? How soon do I want to be happy, joyous, and free?

—Herb Kaighan

Note: Herb Kaighan was given the gift of freedom from alcohol on February 21, 1984. As the result of the application of the Twelve Steps as contained in the *AA Big Book*, he experienced a profound spiritual awakening in 1988. Since then, he has been carrying the message of recovery through books, presentations, facilitating workshops, and leading retreats. He is the author of *Twelve-Step Guide to Using the Alcoholics Anonymous Big Book* (2004), *Twelve Steps to Spiritual Awakening: Enlightenment for Everyone* (2010), and *Practicing the Here and Now: Being Intentional with Step 11* (2017).

Introduction

The *Alcoholics Anonymous Big Book* (2002) states clearly that resentments are the number one reason people fail in recovery. It says, "Resentment is the number one offender. It destroys more alcoholics than anything else. A person mired in resentment has scant chances of recovering from addiction." The ubiquity of resentments and the danger they pose to sobriety make the work of forgiveness essential to recovery.

Our motivation for writing this book stems from our personal struggles to find a constructive response to these questions: What do you do when your life falls apart? And, what if you contributed to its falling apart? It took each of us a long time to find the answer: forgiveness. We truly struggled to learn what South African archbishop Desmond Tutu said so eloquently is true, that "there can be no future without forgiveness" (1999).

We write this book to offer you a proven prescription for releasing resentments, one that has been refined through studies and research conducted over twenty-five years by top researchers and institutions. The resource we offer you is *forgiveness*. If you are worried that we are going to tell you to just "forgive and forget," or to "just get over it already," take heart. We will not simply ask you "to let it go" or "move on." Instead, we will show you what we have learned about how to move forward—*really move forward*—from resentments and the haunting echoes of regret and remorse that debilitated our lives.

Simply put, resentment involves arguing with your past. It means blaming someone else for the mess your life is in. Resentment is a dangerous way to avoid responsibility for our behavior and choices. As writer Elizabeth Gilbert (2006) puts it in *Eat, Pray, Love*, "As smoking is to the lungs, so is resentment to the soul; *even one puff is bad for you*."

If this statement is true, that even one resentment puff is bad for you, then we all need resources for letting them go. Resentments, regrets, and remorse—these are the three r's of "stinking thinking," the toxic stew that hinders our healing and recovery. Stinking thinking and other negative emotions, such as anger, fear, and jealousy, add to the significant challenges of reclaiming one's life from patterns of substance misuse. It is hard enough to relinquish the problems of substance dependence without the extra challenge of resentment, blame, and bitterness.

The Stanford Forgiveness Project

Our research is the product of the Stanford Forgiveness Project (SFP), whose nine steps to forgiveness have been used successfully throughout the world. The project methodology emerges from research projects large and small, handling grievances from insults to murder, and is derived from samples in multiple parts of the world. Dr. Luskin serves as its cofounder and director.

While the forgiveness work was born through rigorous research on the emotional and physical health benefits of forgiveness, our motivation for teaching came out of painful and significant personal life challenges. Each of us had a need to reclaim our own lives from the painful tyranny of grievance, resentment, and regret.

About Dr. Frederic Luskin

I (Frederic) struggled to make peace with a close friend's betrayal, which prompted me to focus my dissertation research on forgiveness. This research eventually led to the personal experimentation and development of the SFP methodology. When the offense occurred I was already a licensed therapist. Yet I was still overwhelmed with how deeply bitter I felt and how long I stayed that way. I was a determined failure at forgiving. At one point my wife turned to me and said she was extremely disappointed in me. She had married me with the expectation that I was more resilient and less negative than I turned out to be. Both my personal struggle and my emotional ineptitude led me to uncover and then research much of what you will find in this book.

My wife's disappointment catalyzed something in me, and the word "forgiveness" popped into view. I recognized the dead end of blame and discovered a bit of gratitude. Slowly and deliberately, I reduced my sense of myself as a victim and took back my power. I finally met with this friend a couple of years later and, we made peace because I had done so already inside. And to this day we continue to be close friends.

After rescuing myself from self-pity, anger, and victimhood, I had to choose a dissertation topic to get a PhD from Stanford University. I decided to do a randomized clinical trial in forgiveness to see if what had worked for me would work for others. My hunch was successful, and the results were compelling and convincing. Forgiveness training reduced anger, stress, and depression, and more significantly, it led to greater hope and inner peace.

Surprisingly, I was only the third researcher in the world to demonstrate that forgiveness was good for physical and mental well-being. Forgiveness had been ignored as an intervention, and there was almost no science attesting to its effectiveness. My dissertation served as a pilot to get funding from the only major grant competition ever awarded for forgiveness research. That grant catapulted the SFP into national prominence and led to the largest randomized trial on the effectiveness of forgiveness psychoeducation.

I have continued to do research and teach what I have learned about forgiveness. My own suffering led me to have empathy for people who are hurt and also to develop a bullshit detector that hears how people choose to stay stuck in victim mode. I had to painfully look at the ways I fooled myself and underestimated my coping and my contribution to my grievances. At this point, I have worked with and helped many thousands of people with grievances large and small.

About Lyndon Harris, MDiv

I (Lyndon) came kicking and screaming to the work of forgiveness. As a former Episcopal priest, I taught forgiveness, preached on forgiveness, and considered myself good with forgiveness. That is, until I had to do the demanding work of forgiveness in my own life. Then I realized just how much I had to learn and how important it was to forgive. Because of fate, I would soon understand just how much my life would require forgiveness to help me heal and move on.

In April 2001, I was chosen by Trinity Church, Wall Street, an Episcopal church in New York City, to develop a new church community at the historic Saint Paul's Chapel, where George Washington had often prayed. Little did I know what kind of church that would become after the terrorist attacks of September 11, 2001, or how great the personal cost.

My long journey to forgiveness began as I stood at the foot of the South Tower of the World Trade Center on the morning of September 11, 2001. I watched it collapse following the impact of a terrorist-hijacked airplane. The next day I returned to the site to assist in the search and rescue mission and to perform last rites on the many bodies recovered. Then, as the minister of the church at the foot of the World Trade Center, I opened the chapel as a support center for first responders. This lasted for eight and a half months. During those months, we served over a half-million meals to first responders.

This mission helped thousands of rescue workers and their families endure the hardships following the attack on the World Trade Center. My service work for weary first responders garnered me national mention and has been widely written about: the *New York Times*, the *Washington Post*, the *Christian Science Monitor*, and *Time* magazine covered this mission. I have been interviewed by CBS News, CNN, MSNBC, and NBC, among others; and covered internationally by BBC Scotland, BBC Ireland, Germany's ARD, and *Die Zeit* (Hamburg).

But there was a catch, another disaster playing out behind the scenes. I felt that I did not get the support I needed from my superiors for this challenging work. I felt there were road-blocks that inhibited what we were trying to do. My growing resentments and the personal conflicts compounded the significant trauma of 9/11. Following the close of the service mission, I landed in a private, but equally intense, personal hell, ultimately losing almost everything I held precious in life. Depression, post-traumatic stress disorder (PTSD), grievances, and multi-ple resentments became my daily bread for over ten years.

Like many 9/11 first responders, I fell apart. I lost my job, left my marriage, borrowed money to rent an apartment I could not afford, and started a nonprofit I could not sustain. Later, I would lose my house in foreclosure and go through the agony of bankruptcy. The pain of these losses was excruciating. I grew increasingly isolated from my friends and support, and my life continued to unravel. I became well acquainted with what the *AA Big Book* (2002) describes as the "three r's of stinking thinking": resentments, regrets, and remorse.

Please do not think forgiveness came easily to me. I started working with the SFP concepts not that long after 9/11, but my resistance was big. Self-pity, shame, and bitterness are not fertile ground for forgiveness. Forgiveness came to me in fits and starts and, like Fred, I know how hard it can be to let go of victimhood and blame. We both are humbled professionals who should have known better and did not. We are also both people who persevered, made course correc-tions, and finally learned to let go of what was holding us back. We are your guides to what we have learned and how these practices and methods from the SFP can help you.

Who This Book Is For

This book is for anyone who wants to learn to forgive. It offers a soup to nuts method for forgive-ness. It takes the processes developed by the SFP and disseminated worldwide through the best-selling book *Forgive for Good* (Luskin 2002) and adapts them as a workbook. Within that big umbrella, the target audience is individuals and family members who have struggled with sub-stance abuse and its recovery. Our research and this workbook are among the first sources to bring research-proven strategies of forgiveness to recovery.

Toward that end, the teaching stories and examples will all be from work we have done with people in recovery and their families. We have learned some of the nuances of forgiveness in recovery from our work, and this book tweaks the forgiveness process in modest ways to speak to those in recovery. Specially, we have dramatically enhanced our exploration of self-forgive-ness to meet the needs of the recovery community.

How to Use This Workbook

We will teach you what forgiveness is and how to do it. We will look at both self-forgiveness and forgiveness of others. This is a workbook, so we provide specific practices for you to use in real time as you go through the book. The book includes practices such as journaling, affirmation, guided imagery, meditation, cognitive disputation, and ways to change your story; some are available for download at http://www.newharbinger.com/53974. In real time, this book will provide you with the methods of the SFP, which have been refined over the past twenty-five years. The chapters are arranged sequentially as we lead you from the beginning of the forgiveness process to its culmination. While you will benefit from reading the introductory chapters to understand the terrain, you do not have to do every exercise in each and every subsequent chapter.

The Forgiveness Journey

In this workbook, we will share what we have discovered on how to respond to life's nos and heartbreaks with a yes to the future through forgiveness. What we learned is that forgiveness is an essential life skill that needs practice—just like throwing a baseball. We learned that forgiveness is a vital strategy for rebuilding your life after tragedy and failure. The practice of forgiveness gave us a road map to navigate the journey from depression and despair to new beginnings, healthier relationships, and greater purpose. Our journey and hard-won new beginnings demonstrate the power of forgiveness to rebuild one's life.

We are not the only people who have made a major life mistake, or been unfairly treated, or lost things very dear. In this workbook we will explore what it means to get a no from life, and we will give you proven, evidence-based strategies for how to respond in ways that are most loving to yourself and to others. It will take us the whole workbook to get there, but we will share with you and explain the hard-won insight that it's better to do good, than feel bad. Better for the world, better for your family, better for yourself. We are not always responsible for what happens to us, but we are responsible for how we respond. In this workbook you will learn proven strategies for responding with creativity, kindness, and self-compassion.

While the strategies in this workbook are useful for any issue of mistreatment or wounding, we focus on those who have struggled with substances. Our examples are from work with people in recovery or their family members or friends. The practices are good for anyone, so a family member can use this book as well.

In some ways we are both here as followers of the adage that those who cannot do, teach. We both failed miserably at forgiving and suffered because of it. Not only have we done some of the research and teaching on forgiveness but we also experienced the abyss of unforgiveness and the desperate need to identify and release our resentments. The path to healing is both difficult and necessary, as we can both attest.

This alchemy of forgiveness research and lived experience is what we will share with you. At the insistence of various treatment and addiction professionals and counselors, we have conducted research through teaching forgiveness to recovery groups and treatment centers for five years. Remarkably, in that time, there was not one single incidence in which a participant (or attending clinician) failed to find the forgiveness work impactful and helpful. The feedback we received in these teaching and research trials has proven invaluable in the ongoing development of this workbook.

Forgiveness is a vital part of many faith traditions and cultures, and there are many different understandings of forgiveness. In this book, we offer a secular research-proven method of forgiveness: the evidence-based SFP forgiveness methodology that has been tested and found impactful for over twenty-five years. We will share with you what forgiveness is and is not, how it works, and why it matters. And we will highlight and expand upon the aspect of forgiveness that research suggests is of utmost importance to people in recovery: self-forgiveness. Forgiveness works. And if you follow the steps in this workbook and incorporate these tools, you will find significant support for developing long-term resilience in your recovery.

Your life is a precious gift, and it is fleeting. None of us know how long we have here or how long we will be healthy. We do not want anyone to waste one more unnecessary day on the grievances that poison us, or the resentments that rob us of peace. Ethicist and theologian Lewis Smedes (1996) said it best: "Forgiveness is setting a prisoner free and discovering, after the fact, that the prisoner was you."

We are both delighted and honored that you have picked up our workbook. We hope and trust that through this work you will find the freedom you deserve.

CHAPTER 1

Forgiveness: What and Why

We strongly advocate the use of forgiveness to help yourself recover from the abuse of substances and heal the resentments that keep you stuck. In clinical and educational settings we have seen the value of forgiveness for both self and others to reduce suffering. In this chapter we will review some of the research that validates the power of forgiveness and highlight research from the Stanford Forgiveness Project (SFP).

Forgiveness as a healing practice has been recommended by nearly every religious and wisdom tradition. For many years it was consigned to the spiritual and religious aspect of life and not considered a part of psychotherapy or research. Only recently have science and research started to affirm the value of forgiveness for physical, emotional, and relationship well-being. Although the SFP is one of only a modest handful of empirically validated forgiveness approaches, on the whole, research suggests that forgiveness is a good practice for overcoming the wounds of the past.

How do you feel about scientific research on forgiveness?

_____

_____

_____

How do you feel about this book being grounded in the research?

_____

_____

Defining Forgiveness

Forgiveness is defined as giving up ideas of revenge and blame, and instead experiencing acceptance and peace, and moving on. Worldwide, religious and spiritual traditions extol forgiveness and have for centuries. The dimming of bitterness and resentment is a normative goal of religious practice. While different faith traditions use different metaphors and language, they generally agree on the value of forgiveness.

The Christian faith is built upon the forgiveness of Jesus as he offers his teaching and is crucified:

"Father, forgive them: for they do not know what they are doing" or "I tell you forgive those who have sinned against you not seven times but seventy times seven times."

Forgiveness is the centerpiece of the Lord's Prayer, a prayer that Jesus asked his followers to pray daily.

The Buddhist forgiveness prayer is:

"If I have harmed anyone in any way, either knowingly or unknowingly through my own confusions I ask their forgiveness. If anyone has harmed me in any way, either knowingly or unknowingly, through their own confusions, I forgive them. If there is a situation, I am not ready to forgive, I forgive myself for that" (Shannon 2008).

The Hindu scripture the Mahabharata states:

"One should forgive under any injury. It has been said that the continuation of the species is due to man's being forgiving. Forgiving is holiness; by forgiveness, the universe is held together. Forgiveness is the might of the mighty; forgiveness is sacrifice; forgiveness is quiet of the mind; forgiveness and gentleness are the qualities of the self-possessed. They represent eternal virtue" (Yogananda 1998).

A Course in Miracles:

"Forgiveness can truly be called salvation. It is the means by which illusions disappear" (Schucman 2007).

Alcoholics Anonymous: Big Book:

"Resentment is the number one offender. It destroys more alcoholics than anything else. From it stem all forms of spiritual disease, for we are not only physically ill we have been spiritually sick. When the spiritual malady is overcome, we straighten out mentally and physically" (*Alcoholics Anonymous* 2002).

Which of these definitions speak to you?

_____

_____

_____

_____

What do you think about a universal belief in forgiveness?

_____

_____

_____

_____

_____

_____

The Case for Forgiveness

While religious traditions go back centuries, it is only since the 1990s that scientific research validated forgiveness. These studies demonstrate the importance that forgiveness can bring to establishing peace of mind and stilling stress in the body. Not only do most of the world's religious traditions advocate for forgiveness, but science also validates it.

Forgiveness is a rich and multidimensional construct, and researching such a construct is not easy. Webb, Robinson, and Brower (2011) assert that one must be aware of the complexity of forgiveness as an intervention:

"Scholarly work on forgiveness defines it as a coping mechanism with unique motivational and volitional qualities… Involving affective, behavioral, and cognitive components…, forgiveness minimally entails the reduction of negative responses to an offender…, yet may also include an increase of positive, love-based emotions… Furthermore, it does not require restitution…, retribution…, or a return to vulnerability, nor does it necessarily involve reconciliation, allowing for offender accountability… Forgiveness is not a denial of justifiable or legitimate negative responses to offense…but an internal process, freely chosen by a victim of offense…, irrespective of subsequent interaction with the offender."

The above is not meant to help you get some sleep while reading this but to remind you that the science of forgiveness is complex. That is why we have faith in what it reveals and why we believe it is important that you know a little about the field and the SFP before you trust us to help you.

How I (Frederic) Discovered Forgiveness

My work as a forgiveness researcher emerged from several experiences I had after my wife told me to shape up. The first was when she sent me to buy something at a local supermarket. As I mentioned previously, the undeserved loss of a close friendship had me in a foul mood, and I was in a job I did not like. Most problematic for me was that I was full of blame and took little responsibility for my emotional status. My wife made clear the specific item she needed was available at only one store and that store was bound to be very crowded as it was around Christmas time.

So cranky me heads off to the store and battles traffic and an overcrowded mall. When I arrived at the spot where the specific item is shelved, the shelf was empty. I was so full of self-pity at that moment that I can only say my brain overheated. Whatever it was, the experience opened me to an experience of grace that I have never forgotten. In my bitterness at my life finding one more obstacle to my happiness, I experienced a simple moment of clarity. I saw that I was in a safe life in a lovely supermarket with a shocking abundance of things to buy. I saw that I was healthy and happily married with a small child, and I was missing it all because I was bitter. Full stop. I am missing it all because I am bitter. This profound lack of attention to the blessings in my own life is not the fault of the person who hurt me. That hurt was in the past, and I am in the present in a supermarket. Ergo, it is up to me whether I see the cup of my life as half full or half empty. What a realization to have at a local supermarket.

I walked out of the mall a partially changed person with my first glimpse into forgiveness. I became much kinder to my wife but still harbored some bitterness over my mistreatment. But an idea had taken hold. If my friend did not ruin my life, why hold on to the past and blame him? I had practiced bitterness and self-pity for so long it was hard to shake the habit, and I still had more to learn.

A few weeks later I am ruminating again about my misfortune, and I begin to have an uncomfortable series of thoughts. I am again cataloging the ways I have been mistreated and reminding myself how I should have been treated better. An uncomfortable realization joined them: I assumed that this friend owed me certain positive behaviors. And then when I did not get those behaviors, I gave myself permission to get and stay mad and hurt. I started to wonder: what if he did not owe me any specific treatment at all? What if the expectation of how he should act was made up in my mind? What if my expectations of him intensified my problem, which meant that my anger was caused by my expectations, not only by what was done to me? What if I could develop a better view of what I am owed and who is responsible for my mental health when I do not get what I want?

It is strange to write that these two simple insights facilitated forgiveness and catalyzed the future direction of my life. Those insights led to the SFP and to the book you are holding in your hand. These insights were sufficient for me to reach back out to the person who hurt me and with a forgiving heart reestablish a successful relationship that endures to this day. Those insights are at the heart of the SFP and the research we will cover in this chapter and book. We are certain that if you can grasp these two insights, they will change your life as well.

Studies on Forgiveness: The Stanford Forgiveness Project

In this section we will review SFP studies that show the effect of forgiveness on a wide range of subjects and issues. My (Frederic's) first study for my dissertation took a sample of fifty-five Stanford students who had an unhealed grudge against someone in their lives. The only parameters were that the offense could not be a violent crime or abuse that happened in the last five years and that the participant could at least imagine at some point forgiving the offender. We took all comers, and the most common offenses were either committed by their parents or their current or past lovers. People admitted to feeling quite hurt by their experience, with the initial rating of hurt around 8.5 on a scale of 1 to 10.

We assessed the participants at the beginning at the training, at the end of the training, and one month past the six ninety-minute sessions of psychoeducation. That means we taught forgiveness not as therapy but as a form of education where folks would learn and practice forgiveness skills. We intend this workbook to be the same: a method of education based on research. The results were strong as participants became more forgiving of their offender, more forgiving in general, and more hopeful and compassionate in their lives.

Our next study is still the largest in-person intervention study of forgiveness. For this project we had 250 participants between the ages of twenty-five and fifty. Again, the results were strongly positive. There were reductions in anger and stress and the physical symptoms of stress. There were improvements in forgiveness of the offender and the general tendency to forgive. In both studies, the participants' rating of how hurt they felt was dramatically reduced and all results remained positive even a month after the forgiveness training had ended.

Our next research was on Catholic and Protestant folks from Northern Ireland who had lost family members or been personally harmed in their long-standing feud. Three times we brought people from both sides of the conflict to spend six days with us, and we taught them how to forgive. One cohort involved a small group of mothers whose sons had been murdered, another was with any person who had a murdered family member, and the third involved people who themselves had been harmed and were now trying to help heal their communities. Because grieving must precede forgiveness we stipulated that anyone there to forgive a murder had to allow two years since the murder to try to forgive.

We have data for the first two cohorts. The small group of mothers showed clear positive gains in forgiveness for what happened. The second group, who had lost any family member to murder, showed reductions in anger, depression, and stress, and improvement in hopefulness. These results, while positive, did not reach statistical significance, which meant that these changes could simply be due to chance.

When we unpacked the results, we found interesting data that demonstrated the importance of carefully measuring change. Out of the seventeen participants, nine showed positive gains in forgiveness, five showed no change in forgiveness, and three showed less forgiveness. Overall, the results were positive for forgiveness of the person who murdered a family member.

We want to acknowledge that forgiveness is not a panacea for all wounds and that people are at different time frames in their healing. It is to be expected that some people confronted with a multi-hour emphasis on the painful loss of a family member might experience more pain and for some the training might not move the forgiveness needle at that point in time. At the same time, it is remarkable that a simple group training could help more than half of the participants forgive the murder of a family member.

The most powerful learning about forgiveness occurred when my Stanford minister partner, Byron Bland, drew a picture on the board and put the word "murder" in a box. He then drew two arrows from the box. One was to family and the other was to community. What he was showing was that both the family and the community had a stake in the murder and often their incentives were at cross-purposes. Sometimes forgiveness is not simply about what happened to you but the cultural context in which it happens.

About ten years later, a forgiveness colleague went to Sierra Leone to conduct an SFP forgiveness and gratitude training as a response to the civil war. Thirty-nine Sierra Leoneans attended a community forgiveness education event in Freetown, the capital city of Sierra Leone. Consistent and large positive changes emerged as the learning modules were taught. A short forgiveness and gratitude community education program in Sierra Leone was able to decrease levels of unforgiveness.

The SFP method has also been adapted to try to reach a variety of different populations. In a comparison-group trial, 104 employees of a large financial services corporation participated in a seven-hour positive psychology intervention with an emphasis on forgiveness. The results were uniformly positive, with increases in positive states, physical vitality, and health-related quality of life, and decreases in stress and anger. Participants also showed a 24 percent increase in gross sales, which was well over double the sales productivity of other employees were in the comparison group.

An SFP–based trial of twenty-five hypertensive patients who completed eight to twelve hours of in-person SFP training showed that improvement in anger expression was greater for the people trained in forgiveness as compared to the control condition. The participants who had high anger scores and hypertension showed significant improvement in their blood pressure. This finding and other forgiveness research suggests that forgiveness can offer positive effects on your cardiovascular well-being.

Finally, the SFP method was compared to a Christian forgiveness method at a small Lutheran college in the Midwest (Toussaint et. al 2020). The six hours of forgiveness classes were taught entirely by undergraduates, and both the SFP and the religious methods were well used by students in the Christian setting. Both unforgiveness and forgiveness were measured pre- and postintervention, and again at a two-month follow-up. Both forgiveness methods led to decreased unforgiveness and increased forgiveness at the end of the six-hour training, and the positive gains were maintained at the follow up assessment two months later.

What is it like for you to read about this research?

_____

_____

Describe any changes in your understanding of forgiveness.

_____

_____

_____

_____

How might forgiveness be good for you?

_____

_____

_____

_____

_____

_____

_____

John's Story

Even though John was a skilled and careful engineer, he really was not the best at doing things that were good for him. Enjoying barbecue, he took seconds when he first went up to the grill so that when he came back for thirds, the optics would not be so terrible. He loved the idea of the exercises recommended by his physician—but not enough to do them. In his mind, when it came to drinking, he did not have a problem, he just had a challenge containing his drinking. Sometimes two beers turned into ten, which were often followed by shots of tequila.

After his heart attack, John had to take a long look at his life. In cardiac rehab, the exercises he was doing incentivized him to look at other problematic areas where he could improve. Deep down, John knew that his drinking was undermining his health. It was damaging his relationships with his wife and daughters. His drinking was not a challenge to be managed as he had naively hoped, but a destructive pattern that was stealing his life. He read in the Big Book that his resentments were dangerous for him, and that the antidote to resentments is forgiveness. A close friend shared some articles on the scientific legitimacy of forgiveness, and John took a class to work on his resentments.

Concluding Thoughts

The research we've discussed leads to a simple conclusion. As people become better able to manage—and ultimately let go of—their grievances, they become less angry and more hopeful that they can better handle their problems and their interpersonal relationships. As they let go of their painful past, the future looks a bit more inviting. Ergo, less stress, anger, and depression, and more hope.

A recent analysis of research demonstrated a strong positive relationship between forgiveness of others and better physical health (Lee and Enright 2019). That means that as you learn to forgive through using this workbook, you will likely get an extra boost in physical well-being.

Now, think back to our work in this chapter. What are the three most important takeaways for you?

1. _____

2. _____

3. _____

CHAPTER 2

The Power of Forgiveness: An Evidence-Based Approach

In 2016, the US Department of Health and Human Services addressed the crisis of substance use disorder (SUD) with an official report. In it, Vivek Hallegere Murthy, then US Surgeon General, sought to promote a focus on finding strategies to address SUD, reminiscent of an earlier Surgeon General's Report about the dangers of smoking over fifty years ago. Murthy states that "substance use disorders represent one of the most pressing public health crises of our time. Whether it is the rapid rise of prescription opioid addiction or the longstanding challenge of alcohol dependence, substance misuse and substance use disorders can—and do— prevent people from living healthy and productive lives. And, just as importantly, they have profound effects on families, friends, and entire communities."

This Surgeon General's Report is also a call to action: "I recognize there is no single solution. We need more policies and programs that increase access to proven treatment modalities. We need to invest more in expanding the scientific evidence base for prevention, treatment, and recovery. We also need a cultural shift in how we think about addiction. For far too long, too many in our country have viewed addiction as a moral failing."

Forgiveness as an Intervention for SUD and Substance Misuse

We believe that forgiveness can be an essential part of long-term recovery. Over twenty years ago, psychologist Everett Worthington and research scientist Michael Scherer (2004) included substance abuse problems as one of many areas of psychological research in health and well-being to which forgiveness would be applicable. In 2007, the then Deputy Director of the National Institute on Alcohol Abuse and Alcoholism argued for the prioritization of research on forgiveness. More recently, scholars have explicitly identified the construct and process of forgiveness in standardized, evidence-based, federally funded treatments for alcohol use disorders (Webb and Trautman 2010).

There is a small body of research that supports the use of forgiveness as an intervention for substance use disorder. Most of the research is of short duration and consists of only a few studies that assess treatment efficacy. The good news is that in almost every study forgiveness is shown to have a positive effect on some aspect of healing. Our two SFP pilot studies in recovery point to the power of forgiveness to enhance recovery and reduce psychological turmoil.

Researchers Webb and Jeter (2015) established that of "…19 of 21 [extant empirical] studies, (90%) suggest that multiple dimensions of forgiveness are meaningful and perhaps essential in addressing problematic substance use." They also claim that forgiveness of self may be the most important aspect in recovery.

Researchers Deane, Wootton, Hsu, and Kelly (2012) examined whether forgiveness of self and others would predict treatment dropout at three months. The examination concluded that forgiveness of self was related to dropping out, while forgiveness of others was not. Simply put, self-forgiveness helped people adhere to recovery.

Researchers Scherer, Worthington, Hook, and Campana (2011) compared the effect of forgiveness of self-intervention against regular recovery care on forgiveness of self, drinking refusal, self-efficacy, and guilt and shame. Those receiving the self-forgiveness intervention showed greater improvements on each of the measures.

Still other researchers—Osterndorf, Enright, Holter, and Klatt (2011)—examined the effect of forgiveness training on forgiving other people on a variety of psychological qualities in a cohort of adult children of alcoholics. The forgiveness treatment had a positive effect on outcomes such as forgiveness of others, self-esteem, depression, and anger.

In a study conducted in Korea, wives of substance abusers were taught how to forgive. The results showed that forgiveness therapy improved the resilience, self-esteem, and spirituality in these wives (Kim and Lee 2014).

The Stanford Forgiveness Project Methods

This is your first glimpse into the methods we use to teach forgiveness. It gives you a road map of what is in the book and offers research that affirms the value of each aspect. The SFP is a forgiveness method that integrates practices from positive psychology, narrative therapy, cognitive disputation, self-regulation, self-forgiveness, and gratitude. In addition to the importance of forgiveness itself in recovery, each aspect of the model is useful for people who are reconsidering the effects of their past. We will briefly describe the parts of the SFP model and their implications on forgiveness for recovery.

Positive Psychology: This is the scientific study of human strength, resilience, and positive traits and emotions. Research shows that increasing positive emotions while reducing negative ones, such as blame and anger, benefits our cardiovascular health and reduces ill health (Tennen and Affleck 1990). Processing and letting go of grievances bring more positive feelings like happiness, satisfaction, and compassion. Forgiveness helps minimize aspects of negative feelings, such as depression, anger, hostility, stress, and distress (Akhtar and Barlow 2018).

Decreasing negative emotions and increasing positive emotions is a win for those in recovery. Forgiveness is understood as an emotional juxtaposition of positive emotions (empathy, sympathy, compassion, or love) against the negative emotions of unforgiveness.

Narrative Therapy: To be successful in forgiving, you need to rewrite your grievance story to reflect a healthier and more resilient understanding, seeing yourself as a successful survivor rather than a helpless victim. Doing this, you reorient the pain, challenge your stinking thinking, and articulate how to let the offense or grudge go. This is the heart of how changing the story helps create forgiveness.

When we cannot do this, we may spend miserable years stuck in a story of victimhood. One of the first victims of the ravages of substance misuse and SUD is the truth. Did you have two drinks? Or ten? Those suffering from SUD are prone to exaggerate or cover up. An article on the webpage of BlueCrest Recovery Center puts it well: "Recognize that lies are often part of the disease of addiction. Addicts lie to fulfill a need, often to protect themselves from pain, humiliation, and the fear that they cannot survive without their addictive substance." SFP teaches that our healing is dependent on our ability to create new and healthier stories.

Cognitive Disputation: Cognitive disputation is challenging the limiting and erroneous beliefs we hold that make us unhappy and angry. A cognitive disputation approach to forgiveness is fundamental to understanding what is causing one's current distress and to offering remediation tools. In the SFP model, unenforceable rules are at the heart of the approach. The primary cause of suffering comes from the thoughts, feelings, and even the physical sensations you have in response to your thoughts about what happened. Understanding our thoughts related to an offense helps us see that we have more options than just being angry, sad, or depressed. Including this step in the forgiveness process is liberating for people in recovery.

In a recent review on the effectiveness of cognitive therapies, the authors state that such therapies are effective in helping people recover from substance abuse (Magill et al. 2019). The limitation is that, as with all substance recovery data, there is the unsolved problem that a sizable number of people relapse.

Self-Regulation: The spiritual traditions exhort their followers to forgive and usually offer a focus on the breath as a helpful meditation practice. Mindfulness meditation cultivates the ability to offer nonjudgmental present-centered awareness. Both are practices in self-regulation, or the ability to control one's thoughts and physical arousal. Forgiveness arises out of developing the capacity to regulate our responses to both personal failings and unmerited wounds inflicted by others. The workbook includes a simple secular breath meditation that enhances the ability to concentrate and to quiet the mind and body. When practiced, meditation leads to increased self-awareness and the ability to make better choices. Both aspects of self-regulation are essential components on the road to recovery.

The Cochrane review of mindfulness as a standalone treatment for substance abuse recovery concluded that mindfulness had only small positive effects (Goldberg et al. 2021). While this suggests it is insufficient as a stand-alone, we believe that it is a necessary component for successful sustained recovery.

Self-Forgiveness: The SFP model asserts that it is more important to do good than feel bad. This assertion is at the heart of self-forgiveness: we need to forgive ourselves and reduce our bad feelings and we also need to make amends when possible. This position is aligned with the Twelve-Step insistence on cataloging wrongs and making amends. SFP method will teach you how to forgive both yourself and others.

The evidence is clear that self-forgiveness is a crucial step in recovery, but often the hardest to attain (Krentzman et al. 2018). Those struggling with self-forgiveness are often challenged by feelings of guilt and shame. Individuals who misuse alcohol may feel emotions such as shame and guilt for destructive behaviors while intoxicated, such as getting a DUI or arguing with a boss or family members. These challenges often may lead to reduced trust within their families or their primary support network, which may cause further friction and conflict, and elevate feelings of guilt and shame (Scherer et al. 2010).

Guilt and shame are two different emotional states. While guilt is focused on an action (for example, *I did something bad*), shame is focused on the person (*I am bad*). While these two states are distinct, it is quite possible that a person can have a combination of the two. In the Stanford methodology, we refer to this combination as "self-attack." Feelings of shame have been found to be detrimental to self-esteem and hopefulness and may increase the propensity to turn to alcohol or drugs to cope with these feelings (Strelan 2007; Yelsma, Brown, and Elison 2002). Shame has been associated with lower levels of self-esteem and higher levels of stress and psychiatric symptomatology, whereas guilt was unrelated to these constructs.

Gratitude: In the SFP methodology, gratitude is a central tenet. Gratitude means having an attitude of thanks that is experienced and expressed. Gratitude and forgiveness are interpersonal strengths that produce well-being through a combination of reflection, positive emotions, and adaptive social behaviors and relationships that facilitate well-being.

Gratitude as a strategy for addressing substance use disorder can be a powerful tool. In a blog post on their website, Lifeskills South Florida (2017) asserts that "cultivating gratitude is an important part of recovery and gratitude is recognized as one of the foundational virtues in the creation of happiness. If individuals are grateful to be on the road to recovery, then it is less likely they will relapse because they are empowered to move forward." Notable gratitude researcher Robert Emmons (2021) states that gratitude can "...lower blood pressure, improve immune function and facilitate more efficient sleep. Gratitude reduces lifetime risk for depression, anxiety, and substance abuse disorders, and is a key resiliency factor in the prevention of suicide. Gratitude is associated with higher levels of good cholesterol (HDL), lower levels of bad cholesterol (LDL), and lower systolic and diastolic blood pressure, both at rest and in the face of stress."

A study on Twelve-Step program members by researchers LaBelle and Edelstein (2018) showed that gratitude was associated with better indicators of recovery. These indicators included following Twelve-Step practices, keeping AA promises, fewer stress and health symptoms, and more post-traumatic growth.

A 2015 study showed that participants in a fourteen-day web-based gratitude intervention developed more positive cognitions (Krentzman et al.). These cognitions aided substance recovery among people attending outpatient treatment for alcohol dependence.

Stanford Forgiveness Project Studies in Recovery

We have conducted the only two studies that directly taught forgiveness as an intervention with people in recovery. The studies are small and the conclusions tentative. Both were led by Lyndon

Harris using materials he derived from our existing forgiveness work. Participants were evaluated at both the beginning and the end of the intervention to see what changes occurred due to the training. In both studies, results showed the value of this work in helping folks with their recovery.

The first pilot was a six-session training held for recovering substance abusers. This small project had nine participants. The forgiveness assessment we used measured both emotional and cognitive aspects of forgiveness. There was a substantial change seen between the first and last session in participants making a decision to forgive. There was also a smaller positive change in feeling the emotions of forgiveness. This study indicates strong positive cognitive impacts from a six-week training and shows a smaller impact on emotional forgiveness, which may require more time to fully develop.

The project showed positive effects in reducing both feelings of distress and unforgiveness while enhancing the general tendency to be forgiving. The amount of distress participants experienced was strongly reduced. Distress and unforgiveness are two negative factors that can not only influence forgiveness and mental health but also worsen substance abuse problems (Worthington 2005). By reducing distress and increasing the tendency to forgive, we know our work will be of value to the reader and can help improve the mental health of folks who want to release their grudges.

The second pilot study was run with six participants. The assessment of participants was more extensive than the first study, and the development of the forgiveness materials was more refined. The most important result was that on two different scales participants showed a significant decline in grievance toward the identified person they entered the study to forgive. Again, there was a huge improvement in the decision to forgive from the beginning of the study to the end. Emotional forgiveness was strongly enhanced while self-forgiveness improved, and participants' emotional distress was reduced.

Sally's Story

Sally was devastated when her husband, Robert, left her for someone else. They had been married for twenty-five years. They had grown distant since their only child left for college. They both developed outside interests in hobbies and social engagements that led them down different paths. Sally's inclination to cocktails had grown steadily from the onset of her empty nest, while Robert's interest in other women also grew. What ensued was the painful uncoupling of two people who hoped they would be together for life.

Sally blamed Robert for everything. That is, until one day she looked at herself in the mirror and saw a woman who drank too much. Had she driven Robert away? Had she been too caught up in her own grief to take notice of his? She blamed herself and pivoted to feelings of shame. How could she have been so blind? What could she do to move forward in her life?

Sally's cousin was a "friend of Bill" (a colloquialism for AA members) and shared with her their lifesaving twelve steps of recovery. Sally got into a group, found a sponsor, and began working the steps. Six months in, Sally found a forgiveness group and let go of the feelings of guilt and shame that had strangled her. Receiving her bronze one-year coin, Sally could see clearly that forgiveness was a life saver.

How about you? Are you ready to begin your journey to forgiveness?

Concluding Thoughts

Our studies suggest that people in recovery can be taught to forgive, can learn to suffer less from their grievances, and can be taught to give up their self-pity and anger. You, the reader, will be coached and inspired to forgive and make progress on both the emotional and cognitive aspect of letting go of your hurts and grudges. Most importantly you will learn to forgive yourself for the mistakes you have made and the damage you have done to yourself and others.

What issues or thoughts arise for you now that might need work?

_____

_____

_____

_____

_____

_____

_____

_____

What are the three most important takeaways for you?

1. _____

2. _____

3. _____

What Forgiveness Is and Is Not

We have often heard that we should forgive, and we have been told that forgiveness is good for us. In fact, we began this book with research showing the benefits of forgiveness. We also pointed out that, from ancient faith traditions to modern psychology, forgiveness ranks highly as being one of the best things we can do for ourselves and others. Unfortunately, knowing that is true is not enough if you, the reader, do not have a clear idea about what forgiveness is, and you have not been told how to do it. We will address both challenges with this workbook.

Understanding Forgiveness

In our experience as forgiveness teachers, participants' misunderstanding of what forgiveness is and is not constitutes one of the biggest hindrances to helping folks. To put it in the positive, an essential part of this book is to help you understand what forgiveness is and how to practice it.

What we know forgiveness *not* to be:

☐ Forgiveness does not condone unkindness.

☐ Forgiveness does not forget that we suffered.

☐ Forgiveness does not excuse bad behavior.

☐ Forgiveness is not an esoteric or religious experience.

☐ Forgiveness does not minimize or deny our pain.

☐ Forgiveness is different from reconciling with the offender.

☐ Forgiveness does not suggest that we suppress our feelings.

☐ Forgiveness is not a substitute for the need for justice.

Place a check mark beside the assertion that resonate with you the most.

Tell why you chose this assertion.

_____

_____

_____

If you disagree with any of these assertions, tell what about the statement you disagree with.

_____

_____

_____

If you've had a personal experience that relates to this assertion, write about it here.

_____

_____

_____

_____

_____

_____

_____

What we know forgiveness to be:

☐ Forgiveness is the peace you feel when you let go of unresolved grievances.

☐ Forgiveness is primarily of benefit to you.

☐ You forgive for your own well-being, not someone else's, even though they too may benefit.

☐ Forgiveness means reclaiming your personal power.

☐ Forgiveness releases the hold you have given the past to make you suffer in the present.

☐ Forgiveness means taking responsibility for how you feel, instead of blaming others for your disordered thinking or feeling.

☐ Forgiveness is a teachable skill, just like learning to play the guitar.

☐ Forgiveness changes your role in your story from a victim to a hero.

☐ Forgiveness is your choice. You do not have to forgive. You choose to.

☐ Forgiveness is available to everyone who wants it.

☐ Everything is forgivable by someone.

Place a check mark beside the assertion that resonates with you the most.

Tell why you chose this assertion.

_____

_____

_____

If you disagree with any of these assertions, tell what about the statement you disagree with.

_____

_____

_____

If you've had a personal experience that relates to this assertion, write about it here.

_____

_____

_____

_____

_____

_____

_____

_____

_____

Let's consider how understanding forgiveness contributes to issues of recovery from addiction. We assert that forgiveness is an essential step for healing and recovery because forgiveness helps the person in recovery process and release negative emotions, such as resentments, regrets, and remorse. We must help you understand what forgiveness is and is not, so you can begin the journey with a destination in mind. We know that sustained recovery is in direct relationship to your ability to forgive, and the first step is to be clear what forgiveness is.

Resentment: A Major Risk Factor for Recovery

Again, as the *AA Big Book* points out, some of the greatest challenges to recovery are feelings of resentment: "Resentment is the #1 challenge for recovery."

And from Project Match's *Twelve-Step Facilitation Therapy Manual* (1999):

Anger and resentment are pivotal emotions for most recovering alcoholics. Anger that evokes anxiety drives the alcoholic to drink to anesthetize it. Resentment, which comes from unexpressed (denied) anger, represents a constant threat to sobriety for the same reason.

According to the literature of recovery, there are three r's of stinking thinking:

- Resentment—simmering anger at having been treated unfairly

- Remorse—deep regret or guilt for a mistake; self-directed resentment

- Regret—a feeling of sadness, repentance, or disappointment over something that has happened

Therefore, if resentments are the #1 reason people in recovery are challenged, then forgiveness is the #1 best tool for recovery because forgiveness is a proven strategy for dealing with resentments. The strength of our model is its capacity to work with anger, resentment, remorse, regret, and shame, working to release and resolve these dangerous negative emotions. Resentments are poison pills for people in recovery. If you are holding resentment, you are working against your recovery.

Now, let's do a resentment exercise.

Exercise: Resentments

Take a couple of slow and deep breaths and ask yourself, *Am I currently harboring any resentments?* Maybe you resent your boss who promoted someone else for the position you wanted. Maybe you still have feelings of resentment toward your spouse for harping about your drinking. What resentments do you have? List three of them. Please be fearless. Your honesty about this will pay off.

_____

_____

_____

Now, pick one of these resentments and let's work with it. Is the resentment "hot"? Does it have a color or texture? Does it linger with you throughout your day? Where do you experience it in your body? Write down your thoughts.

_____

_____

_____

_____

_____

_____

_____

_____

How might your life be different if you were able to let this resentment go?

_____

_____

_____

_____

_____

What makes you hesitate about letting it go?

_____

_____

_____

We all know that you cannot go in two directions at the same time. Are you heading toward your resentments or toward your recovery?

Another way to address these concerns is to ask yourself, *Where am I stuck?*

On any given day, any one of us might be traveling around with many different challenges or irritations. Some trivial: your shirt has a stain that you did not notice before you left for work, your umbrella is at home and it just started pouring, or your coffee came with milk in it and you prefer it black. Some challenges are not so trivial: your boss just wrote you up for being late again, your kid is in trouble at school, or your spouse cheated on you.

Whether large or small, every one of us carries around disappointment and difficulty. And if you are in the recovery community you might have additional challenges: the dangerous temptation to drink when you get bad news, or perhaps painful reminders of relationship tensions or bridges burned in the past.

Think of yourself as being stuck on the monkey bars when you were a kid on the playground. The only way to move forward and get to the other side is to let go of the bar behind you and reach for the one in front of you. We are here to help you do that with forgiveness.

The Painful Side of Life—Receiving an Arrow to the Heart

In *Taking the Arrow Out of the Heart*, poet Alice Walker (2018) wrestles with the painful side of life, likening it to receiving an arrow to the heart. The truth is that no one escapes the tragedy of an arrow to the heart; it is a part of our shared humanity. And even if you live a blessed and peaceful long life, at some point you will face the stark reality of the human condition: death. As author Nanea Hoffman (2023) observes, "the biggest problem with life is that none of us is going to get out alive!" There is no escaping the reality that at some point in life an arrow of sorrow, or anger, disappointment, or despair will pierce your heart. It is just a part of the balance of life. While there are moments of sublime beauty and love, there are also tragic experiences that will break our hearts.

When we get an arrow to the heart, our first response is to say, *That hurts!* or *Why did this have to happen to me?* This reaction is natural and healthy. But if after twenty years we are still asking *Why did this happen to me?* we are not living our best life. And very likely we need to do some forgiving.

The Painful Side of Life: Getting a No

After years of teaching and reflection we came to a very simple definition of forgiveness. We think of it now as the process of making peace with the word "no"—making peace with those arrows to the heart, making peace with life's heartaches and disappointments.

People would come to our classes and say, "My partner lied to me." Or "My partner cheated on me." Or "My partner is drunk again." Or "I did the stupidest thing." Everyone had a yes they wanted to have happened, and they came to forgiveness classes because they could not make peace with the no they received. You wanted *this*, but life gave you *that*. Or you did not want this, but life gave it to you anyway. And to be sure, life's nos can be wide-ranging—some small and insignificant, and some tragic. Some are minimal: you really wanted the chicken salad sandwich, but they ran out, so you got the pimento cheese instead. At the other extreme, some nos are devastating—like the loss of a loved one in an automobile accident. No to the promotion. No to an extension on your rent. No to your prayers to save your father from cancer. No to your own prayers to save *yourself* from cancer. The word "no" can be hard to hear. For folks in recovery getting a no can translate into *Poor me. Poor me. Pour me a drink.*

Life offers many responses to receiving a no from life or getting an arrow to the heart: anger, depression, resentments, substance misuse, and so on. But the healthiest long-term strategy is to choose to accept and to forgive. Something happened to you that you did not want, and it is important. It had a profound effect on your life. Getting insight into what that is helps you process your feelings about it. In treating clients dealing with negative emotions, therapists often encourage them to "name it before we can tame it" or "feel it before we can heal it." Doing this will empower your sobriety and recovery, and open pathways for you to enjoy living a better life. Forgiveness is learning the skill of removing arrows, bee stingers, and splinters that enter our lives unwanted and then remain long past the time they have any value. The initial sting of these painful experiences tells us that we need to find help, or to protect ourselves from further harm.

To think that we should never have to face pain or difficulty is to misunderstand how precarious, precious, vulnerable, and beautiful the gift of life is. If you have spent twenty years bemoaning how you were slighted, you are not living a joy-filled life. And, unfortunately, the responsibility for that is on you.

Forgiveness as It Relates to the Pain of Life

Every one of us will receive nos from life and arrows to the heart, but through forgiveness we are able to grieve and process our misfortune—whatever it is. Even if, God forbid, there is a debilitating automobile accident, or the loss of a limb from an explosion in war, there still can be a quality of life—provided we are intentional about creating it. There are many inspiring stories of soldiers returning from war wounded who then seize the opportunities that awaited them, instead of giving in to the prison of self-pity and despair.

If you are still breathing, an arrow to the heart, whether self-inflicted due to a mistake you made, or at the hand of another person or life event, is recoverable. Likewise, a no from life does not have to be the final word. The recovery literature is clear about the importance of a fearless moral inventory and the need to make amends if necessary.

Is Everything Forgivable?

To say that everything is forgivable is a bold assertion, and it is important for you to hear this from us at the outset. If there is something you need to forgive, or if you need to ask for forgiveness or to forgive yourself for a mistake you made, all of this is possible. Why? Because, in our approach, forgiveness is something we do for ourselves. When you forgive, it in no way suggests the perpetrator should not be held accountable.

To the person who did you harm, you can spend your life saying "I hate you" or "I despise you" or some words like these. It is your life; it is your choice. Unfortunately if you choose to be miserable, that is on you. If you spend your life talking about how much you hate the other person, you will not have the time or the creative emotional energy to express your love to your family and friends, and to live your life to the fullest.

The Cost of Unforgiveness

Unforgiveness, whether toward others or toward yourself, is a toxic cocktail that is a threat to your sobriety. Arguing that you should have gotten a yes when you got a no for ten years is exhausting. It is also a little crazy to think your opinion of how life should turn out different will have any effect other than making you tired and angry. It is also sad to see grown men and women arguing that life did not turn out the way they wished as they stay stuck in the past.

Now, let's do some exercises.

Exercise: Arrows to the Heart

Bring to your mind an arrow to the heart or a no from life you have received. Some examples might be "My partner cheated on me" or "My mother was abusive" or "My boss blamed me for someone else's mistake" or "I cannot drink like everyone else and that is not fair."

The reason we ask you to name your arrow, your no, or where you are stuck, is so that we can begin processing the experience and prepare to release it through forgiveness.

Echoing the inventory of resentments exercise earlier, the first step in the forgiveness process is to get clear about what happened and what you feel about it. This forgiveness process works for offenses both big and small.

Think of some arrows to your heart or a no you got from life. Write down up to five.

_____

_____

_____

_____

_____

Choose one that has a good deal of energy but not an overwhelming amount; that is, something you can work with, not something that will strongly upset you just by thinking of it. Put a check mark next to it.

On a scale from 1 to 10 (with ten being the most painful), where would you rate this experience?

_____

Why did you rate it that way?

_____

_____

How often do you think about this experience? In what situations?

_____

_____

_____

_____

_____

What do you typically do when you think about this experience?

_____

_____

Exercise: The Serenity Prayer

Now, relax, take a few breaths, and just sit for a moment. Let's look at the Serenity Prayer. Quietly say it to yourself:

> *God, grant me the serenity to accept the things I cannot change, the courage to change the things I can, and the wisdom to know the difference.*

The prayer distinguishes between two things: the things you can change or control, and the things you cannot change or control.

So much of our life is spent trying to change the things we cannot change; that is, getting a no and wanting a yes, or getting a yes and wanting a no. Unfortunately, we have very little power to change much of anything that has already happened. That is, we have little to no influence over the past. Do you agree with that idea? Why or why not?

_____

_____

_____

_____

_____

_____

_____

_____

Our predicament becomes especially tricky when the thing we try to change is other people's behavior in the past. Goodness knows, I (Lyndon) have tried. I finally was able to appreciate the wisdom of Lily Tomlin's quotation, "Forgiveness means giving up all hope of a better past"

(Goldstein 2010). Psychologist James R. Sherman (1982) took it one step further: "We can't change the past, but we can start where we are and change the future."

What do you think about this?

_____

_____

_____

What are one or two things about your past you wish you could change?

_____

_____

_____

Trying to change something that you cannot control is an exercise in futility; it can paralyze you emotionally and affect your physical well-being. Why is it good to let these things go?

_____

_____

Our process of forgiveness is simple, but it is not easy. Are you willing to try? Write a declarative statement of your intention. Here's an example: "I choose the path of forgiveness for myself so that I may live a happier life and strengthen my recovery."

_____

_____

_____

Are you willing to start where you are and see if you can change your future? Explain your response.

_____

_____

_____

_____

_____

What hopes do you have for your future? List three concrete goals for a relationship you cherish or a plan of action to live your life to the fullest.

1. _____

2. _____

3. _____

Important: We are not asking you to give up negative feelings; we are asking that you open your heart to the reality that your life is bigger than a no, a regret, a mistake, a rejection, or a tragedy.

There are three kinds of forgiveness:

1. Interpersonal forgiveness—forgiving someone else

2. Self-forgiveness—forgiving actions we have committed

3. Existential forgiveness—forgiving "life" or our higher power for our problems or suffering

What type of forgiveness challenges are you dealing with?

_____

_____

_____

Choosing to Forgive

In *The Sun Does Shine: How I Found Life and Freedom on Death Row*, Anthony Ray Hinton (2018) has no time to waste on resentments. Wrongfully accused of murder, Hinton spent thirty years of his life on death row in Alabama until he was exonerated. He writes, "I chose to forgive. I chose to stay vigilant to any signs of anger or hate in my heart. They took thirty years of my life. If I could not forgive, if I could not feel joy, that would be like giving them the rest of my life. The rest of my life is mine. Alabama took thirty years. That was enough."

Hinton discovered the hard way that if he continued to focus on the hatred he had for the injustice he faced, he would not have the quality of life he wanted. And without a doubt, if you choose to focus on your resentments, you will not have the best quality of life that is possible for you, either. In fact, every time you express your outrage over the nos in your life, whether outwardly or within, your body suffers, and you do not allow your mind to rest. Think about this: just because someone hurt you in the past does not mean that the rest of your life needs to be a reminder of that experience. Forgiveness empowers us to process the hurt and to release it.

While forgiveness is not linear, each step of our forgiveness methodology is important: it builds on what has come before. This staircase will help you keep track of where you are on your journey to forgiveness competency and understanding; you can download a copy at http://www.newharbinger.com/53974.

Self-Heal

HEAL

Self-Forgiveness

Your Forgiveness Story

Positive Intention

Unenforceable Rules

Change the Channel

PERT

Gratitude

Revenge Fantasies

Stop Taking Things Too Personally

Grievances

What Forgiveness Is and Is Not

Simple Affirmations

Evidence shows that we reinforce what we learn by emphasizing and repeating to ourselves our positive commitments and attitudes. Please repeat one or more of these affirmations to yourself now to center yourself in the healing path of forgiveness. It is also helpful to remind yourself through affirmation of positive decisions you are making. To keep these affirmations at hand, you can download them at http://www.newharbinger.com/53974.

- I deserve to forgive and be forgiven.

- Forgiveness is something I do for myself.

- Forgiveness supports my sobriety and enhances my recovery.

- To forgive is my choice alone.

You can use these lines to add your own affirmations.

_____

_____

Concluding Thoughts

We have now introduced you to our model: what forgiveness is and is not, how forgiveness interfaces with one of the basic predicaments of being human—we want a yes and we get a no in a way that feels like an arrow to the heart. The human predicament is our vulnerability to such wounds and our inability to make peace with our wounds. We reminded you that wounds that lead to resentment are dangerous for people in recovery because they threaten your sobriety and peace of mind.

If there are sections in the chapters you've read so far that remain a challenge for you, write about them here.

_____

_____

_____

_____

_____

_____

_____

_____

Write down three key takeaways that stand out for you in this chapter.

1. _____

2. _____

3. _____

CHAPTER 4

Grievances and Revenge Fantasies

Let's look at how a grievance develops and the accompanying desire for revenge that many struggle with. We will normalize the desire for revenge—not saying everyone should have revenge fantasies but acknowledging that most of us do. By becoming aware of this, we can process these desires in healthy, constructive ways, and not make the common mistake of acting on them. We will emphasize an underappreciated problem with revenge: there is no future in it. Popular books and movies often show the glory of a good payback. Fortunately, in the real world, revenge is rarely so effective or helpful. When you are in recovery, you do not have the bandwidth to manage both your recovery and the distraction of useless revenge ideas.

Are You Held Hostage by Your Grievance Story?

If you are telling a grievance story, you are living in the past, not the present. By doing so you assume the role of victim. Do you know what the biggest problem with being a victim is? You give up your power. You surrender your agency, the privilege of overseeing your life. Instead of being a victim in someone else's story, we want you, through forgiveness, to become the hero of your own life, the protagonist of your own story. There is an enormous difference between these two approaches. For example, instead of saying "_____ did this to me and it cost me a lot," you might say, "This happened to me, and it was bad. But I learned a lot about myself, and I found a new way to move forward in my life."

Here is a test we have designed to look at whether the story you are telling qualifies as a grievance story.

Have you told your story more than twice to at least three different people?	Y	N
Do you replay in your mind the events that happened multiple times a day?	Y	N
Have you made an unsuccessful commitment to tell the story without getting upset?	Y	N
Is the person who wounded you the main character of your story?	Y	N
Do you often negatively speak in your mind to the person who hurt you?	Y	N
When you tell this story does it remind you of other difficult life experiences?	Y	N
Does your story center on what was wrong and how you have suffered?	Y	N
Is your story more about the past than the present?	Y	N
Have you made an unsuccessful commitment to yourself to not tell the story again?	Y	N
Do you look for other people with similar problems to share your story?	Y	N
Do you look for new people to tell your story to?	Y	N
Have you carefully checked the story for accuracy?	Y	N

If you answered yes to five or more of the first eleven questions and/or no to the last question, there is a good chance you are telling a grievance story. Now we will let you know what the problem with that is.

From Grieving to Grievance

When we get an arrow to the heart, our first response is to cry out in pain. That is normal—it hurts. Some of our pains may last a long time while others will be short-lived. The hard question to answer is, what do we do after the wounding? One temptation is to turn our healthy grieving process into a grievance. Grief is necessary. With loss and mistreatment our brain and nervous system need time to digest the suffering and adjust to a changed world. Grief is that period of disruption, pain, and turmoil as we move through loss and change.

Unfortunately, we often look for someone or something to blame for our suffering, and when we do that, we run the risk of creating a grievance. When we create a grievance, which often short-circuits legitimate grief, we can waste years complaining how unfair whatever we experienced was. We cry out to the universe about how much we are already dealing with, and how wrong it is that *this too* happened to us. We compare the arrow in our heart to the arrow in someone else's heart, typically finding that our suffering is worse.

When we develop a grievance, it is usually directed toward someone else, or life, in the form of resentment. Or if, in the case of a self-inflicted emotional wound, we direct the negative energy toward ourselves in the form of regret and/or feelings of remorse. Our anger toward others for treating us poorly, or toward ourselves for mistakes made, can be a healthy initial response.

The first thing we need to do when we get an arrow to the heart is to remove it. The longer we let it fester, the harder it is to deal with it. We remove the arrow by identifying and dismantling our grievances and resentments. This is more easily said than done. But it is possible, and we have tools that can help you do this.

Identifying and Understanding a Grievance

A grievance starts when two things happen in sequence: (1) something occurs in our lives that we did not want to happen, and (2) we deal with this disappointment by a predictive set of responses that make the disappointment take up way too much negative space in our heads.

Another way of saying this is when something happens that we did not want to have happen, we often exaggerate the problem by making it too personal. We cry out in pain because it is about us. They meant to hurt us. We are blameless victims.

That cry is fine when grief begins, but left unchecked it can lead to problems. When something unwanted happens, it is only natural that we make certain assumptions. We may make assumptions about the other person and their motivation. If we get cut off in traffic, we assume the other driver is a jerk. Or incompetent. Or that we played no part in creating the problem. Which may be the case. It is possible that he is a jerk who was out to get us. But isn't it also possible that the other driver could have been a pediatric surgeon called in to perform emergency surgery? Or someone who was in a hurry and had no consciousness of us at all? The bottom line is, we do not know.

When we take things too personally, we make assumptions that make a difficult situation worse. The creation and then repetition of our all-about-us victim narrative wreaks havoc on us mentally and physically, and our personal power goes down the drain. This experience is now a threat to our sobriety rather than just simply coping as best we can with getting a no. It is very important to remember that most people do things that hurt others out of indifference rather than bad intentions. The sad reality is we matter too little, not too much.

You may be thinking, *It was me who was cut off in traffic, so how could it not be personal?* What we want to illuminate in this section is: yes, the incident did happen to you, and that is personal, but are we the only ones ever to be cut off in traffic? No. To have a heart attack? No. To suffer a lover's betrayal? No. When we take things too personally, we run the risk of thinking that we are the only people who have ever suffered in this way. And thus, our wounded ego longs for revenge when the other two parts of the grievance come to join the party. In addition, we assume that the person who hurt us wanted to hurt us, and not that they were indifferent to our suffering. We have found the overwhelming reason people hurt others is selfishness and indifference. In *The Four Agreements: A Practical Guide to Personal Freedom*, Don Miguel Ruiz (1997) declares that the second agreement is not to take things personally:

"Whatever happens around you, do not take it personally… Nothing other people do is because of you. It is because of themselves. All people live in their own dream, in their own mind; they are in a completely different world from the one we live in. When we take something personally, we assume that they know what is in our world, and we try to impose our world on their world.

Even when a situation seems so personal, even if others insult you directly, it has nothing to do with you. What they say, what they do, and the opinions they give are according to the agreements they have in their own minds…Taking things personally makes you easy prey for these predators, the black magicians. They can hook you easily with one little opinion and feed you whatever poison they want, and because you take it personally, you eat it up…."

Do you agree or disagree with Ruiz's statement? Tell why.

_____

_____

_____

_____

Think of a recent situation where you know you took an experience too personally. What was the experience?

_____

_____

_____

How did you overpersonalize it?

_____

_____

_____

How could you have responded a little less personally?

_____

_____

_____

_____

In every issue we face, we have a personal subjective response and an impersonal objective response. The goal is to find a healthy balance between personal and impersonal. There is value in the subjective (what it feels like from your perspective) *and* the objective (what the facts are). But if you focus only on one, you will not heal.

The Blame Game

The next step in forming a grievance is to blame the offender for your emotional, mental, and physical reactions. *It is their fault I am a mess. It is their fault that I am depressed.* After taking it too personally we create another set of unproven assumptions around whose fault and responsibility our lives are. Blame holds out the hope that dealing with and recovering from an offense may not be our responsibility.

Think about an unforgiven experience. Pinpoint one person, group or event that hurt you.

_____

_____

_____

Think about the consequences this hurt has had on your life. List three things that have negatively impacted your life because of the grievance.

_____

_____

_____

Write down your blame hypothesis. (A blame hypothesis is the story of how it is their fault that we are still suffering.)

_____

_____

_____

When you are knee-deep in blaming, how does this make you feel, both physically and emotionally?

_____

_____

_____

Next, think of a modest issue you have dealt with recently, something you would rate a 4 or 5 on a scale of 1 to 10. It could be something as simple as getting irritated with the person who gives you misleading customer service when you are in a hurry to get to an appointment. Or perhaps someone hit your car while you were driving to work, but there was no real damage to your car.

Pick one grievance and write it down here.

_____

_____

_____

Now, take a moment to express how you felt; for example, "I was angry" or "I was scared."

_____

_____

List the thoughts you had about the experience.

_____

_____

Next, write down what you did in response; for example, "I gave him the finger," "I caught up to him and cut him off in traffic," "I gave her a piece of my mind."

_____

_____

_____

Place a check mark beside any of your feelings, thoughts, or actions that *positively affected the outcome*. In what way they were effective?

_____

_____

_____

Now look at all the responses you did not check. Pick one or two and describe how they had no positive impact.

_____

_____

_____

_____

Were there more items checked or unchecked? Share any thoughts that come up for you now.

_____

_____

_____

How much time do you spend brooding over something painful or negative that has happened to you? When you think about those events, how intense are the associated emotions? If you envision your mind as a house, ask yourself, *How much space am I renting out to the grievance?* How you answer these questions will let you know if you are renting too much space in your head to bad tenants.

Let's focus on a simple scenario of getting cut off in traffic, and see how its negativity can spill over. This happens to us, and we are frightened. It is dangerous; we could have had an accident. We have an angry response and then we hang on to our anger, taking what happened too personally. We blame someone for the response of our mind and body and are filled with negative assumptions and nasty stories. In a clinical understanding, it is not the actions of another that cause us to feel bad. When someone does something we do not like, we respond emotionally by getting upset or angry. Our bodies respond physiologically: our heart rate increases, our blood pressure increases, our nervous system dumps stress chemicals into our bodies, and we can be a mess.

It is not accurate to say something like "You made me feel that way." Someone does something we do not like, and our bodies respond because of our displeasure. This is such an important truth. Studies have shown that it does not matter if the negative thing happened two days ago or twenty years ago, if we do not work to process the experiences and to regulate our bodies, the same detrimental response will continue to occur.

For example, when something negative happens on the way to work (such as missing a train), all too often we take that energy with us into the workplace. Imagine that the boss is critical of something you did the day before and you arrive on edge, angry about the morning commute. You respond to her criticism by getting defensive, which can make for a tense exchange with your boss. The ripples from this interaction can bounce from person to person in the department. This is not a winning scenario for health and happiness, or career longevity. Think of forgiveness as a kind of spiritual aikido, a martial art focused on self-care and thriving.

Now let's do another practice. Think of a more meaningful grievance you have that remains unresolved—perhaps 6 or 7 on a scale of 1 to 10.

What is the grievance?

_____

_____

_____

Who harmed you and in what way?

_____

_____

_____

What are the consequences of the problem that you still face?

_____

_____

Write down any thoughts you had that might have made the situation extra personal.

_____

_____

_____

How do you feel when it becomes a personal insult?

_____

_____

Give an example of blame that might be exchanged by you taking responsibility for your emotions and thoughts in the present. (For example, *I might not have gotten that promotion because I had not yet completed training that would have enhanced my candidacy.*)

_____

_____

_____

Try to imagine a less charged and blaming way to describe the situation. Write down your thoughts.

_____

_____

_____

Breaking the Cycle of Revenge

Many of us harbor thoughts of revenge, not forgiveness. These thoughts are natural. The smartest thing to do when we have a grievance is to pull out the arrow, acknowledge that it hurt, and find a way to make peace with the no—but we do not always do the smartest thing first.

What typically happens for many of us when we get hurt is that we scheme, we find a way to get even. To make the other person "pay." We look for ways to get revenge. This is natural, and we are hard-wired for this response. Everett Worthington (2006), a forgiveness researcher, says that when we contemplate revenge the pleasure centers in the brain light up—the same ones that light up when we eat chocolate! That's why revenge is often referred to as "sweet revenge."

A key component of forgiveness is to examine, interrogate, and process these revenge fantasies. A revenge fantasy is that secret desire we all have, when someone treats us poorly, to pay them back. But, as we stated, the biggest problem with revenge is there is a limited future in it. Whether it is getting even with a coworker or the insufferable legacy of the Hatfield–McCoy feud, we are consumed with negative emotions that have potentially destructive outcomes. Forgiveness is breaking the cycle of revenge.

Most of us have our grievance story at easy recall. Even if we bury the hatchet, we sometimes keep a detailed map to know where exactly to dig it up. When we suffer an offense—someone cuts us off in traffic, our boss takes credit for our idea, a lover betrays us, a friend lies to us—it is natural that we may be hurt or become angry. Often because there is no good outlet for our anger, and we do not like how vulnerable that makes us, we linger with our revenge fantasy.

Constructive and Destructive Anger

There are two types of anger: constructive and destructive. Constructive anger can save your life. If you find yourself or a loved one attacked, the adrenalin from your anger response generates your innate capacity to fight and protect, or to flee quickly. Also getting angry over being passed over for a promotion or an opportunity can generate the inspiration needed to formulate an alternative plan for your success. These are constructive examples of anger.

On the other hand, anger can be quite destructive. Prolonged anger festers into hostility which becomes a dangerous risk factor in heart attacks. If you hold on to your anger for too long, it will consume you. The Buddha said, "Holding on to anger is like grasping a hot coal with the intent of throwing it at someone else; but you are the one who gets burned."

It is essential for our sobriety and fulfillment in life to manage our anger. After the initial experience of anger, it helpful for us to take a minute and examine the anger to determine its usefulness. Because we do not like the bitter pill of acceptance and because we have not learned to forgive, the temptation is to hold on to our anger indefinitely. And when we are angry or hostile, we will not make our best or most constructive decisions. But because we do not know how to make peace with a no from life, and because we do not like the vulnerability that is revealed to us when we are hurt, anger can become destructive.

Unmanaged destructive anger often leads to a desire for revenge. Since we have all been hurt or disappointed when life did not give us what we want, each of us has ruminated on revenge at one time or another. It is important to acknowledge the normalcy of this, and then perhaps share these fantasies with a trusted friend or two. It is better to share a revenge fantasy about getting even than to act on it. No matter the content, when we locate and talk about these revenge fantasies, we can shrink their intensity and reach a deeper understanding of our grief beneath the bluster.

Revenge Fantasies

Sit quietly, turn off your cell phone, and relax. Take a couple of slow and deep breaths to prepare for this exercise. Then recall a recent grievance that still gets under your skin, one that still rankles you.

Describe the offense in some detail. What happened? Who caused the incident?

_____

_____

_____

_____

_____

_____

What was the no you got?

_____

What was the yes you wanted?

_____

In what way did you take what happened personally?

_____

_____

In what way did you blame the offender for how you felt?

_____

_____

What lingering negative emotions or resentments do you still carry?

_____

_____

Describe your thoughts of revenge.

_____

_____

_____

_____

_____

Acknowledging revenge desires helps us get clear that acting on them would be a bad idea. List possible repercussions to acting out your fantasy.

_____

_____

_____

What, if any, benefit do you gain from having this revenge fantasy?

_____

_____

Describe any cost to this fantasy.

_____

_____

Revenge fantasies sometimes compensate for deeper feelings of vulnerability and insecurity. For example, when you are in pain from something that happens—say, a friend betrays you—your response to "make him pay" is more than just settling the score. It could also be about the insecurity we feel when we acknowledge that we live in a world where close friends can betray us. It is about the fact that we live in a world where—if we are paying attention—we must acknowledge that we are vulnerable, limited, and at the mercy of things beyond our control. For folks struggling with substance misuse, one way to get revenge on someone who never stops harping about our drinking is to keep drinking.

Also helpful in understanding and dismantling our revenge fantasy is to consider how the current pain might be related to other pains we have suffered. Our current offenses can be magnified by previous similar offenses. Often, there can be an accumulative effect from past grievances. For example, getting cut off in traffic can trigger us in ways that connect to unresolved anger and pain for all the ways we have been cut off in life, or ways in which our plans have been thwarted by another.

It is often those unforgiven past hurts that make our lives difficult today. Sometimes we get upset over a small slight and wonder why we got so bent out of shape.

Living Well Is the Best Revenge

We want to finish the chapter by emphasizing that there is one revenge strategy we highly recommend: living well. A life well lived is the best revenge. This often heard but rarely practiced aphorism contains a simple truth. The best way to get over something is to move on and live one's life as fully as possible. End of story. Simple to aim toward, not so easy to pull off.

What does this truth mean to you?

_____

_____

_____

_____

How might you have applied it to a grievance in the past?

_____

_____

_____

_____

How might this idea motivate you today?

_____

_____

_____

_____

What is one action step you already take to live well?

_____

_____

What is one commitment you can make to yourself to work toward a better future?

_____

_____

A Cautionary Tale: Carl Ericson and Norman Johnson

"The man standing at Norman Johnson's door that cold January evening was a stranger who might have seemed vaguely familiar. Johnson, a retired high school instructor who taught English and coached tennis and football for 35 years in this unassuming town[Madison, SD], probably didn't even have his door locked when he came to greet the bearded, gray-haired visitor. The man bluntly asked him, "Are you Norm Johnson?"

When the 72-year-old Johnson did not answer quickly enough, the man asked again. When Johnson finally said yes, the intruder shot him twice in the face, leaving him to die on the doorstep of his tidy brown-clapboard home" (Glionna 2012).

The tragedy of this story began over fifty years earlier. Carl Ericsson was the manager for the high school football team. He would help organize practices, serve as a gofer for coaches, and do the laundry for the team. After one victorious game, the star athlete, Norm Johnson, decided to have a little fun at Ericsson's expense: he placed his sweaty shorts over Carl's head, and everyone had a laugh at Carl's expense.

For more than fifty years, Ericsson nursed a desire for revenge based on a grudge from that night. Fifty years ago—a conflict that festered and hurt two lives.

Simple Affirmations

As you read in Chapter 3, repeating affirmations will reinforce what you have been learning about forgiveness. To make it easy to access these affirmations, you can download them at http://www.newharbinger.com/53974.

- It is okay to feel angry when I do not get what I want.

- I am not a prisoner of my past.

- I can release my anger.

- Forgiveness enables me to live fully in the present.

- Forgiveness allows me to release negative feelings that threaten my sobriety.

Create your own affirmation here.

_____

_____

_____

Concluding Thoughts

The cautionary tale you just read is an extreme example of an out-of-control revenge fantasy. We exhort you to not let a desire for revenge consume your life. Move on and live as fully as you are able. Entertain the revenge idea long enough to disregard it as a good strategy, stop blaming the world for not treating you as you wished, and learn to forgive. The rest of this book will teach you our specific practices for moving on and letting go so you can work with—and not against—your sobriety.

Looking back at this chapter, what are the three most important takeaways for you?

1. _____

2. _____

3. _____

CHAPTER 5

The Healing Balm of Gratitude

To us this is the most important chapter in the book. Here we explore the importance of gratitude for a life of forgiveness, health, and sobriety. We will consider what gratitude is and the benefits of becoming more grateful.

Gratitude is essential for both forgiveness and recovery; in fact, gratitude and appreciation are antidotes for grievances. Appreciating your life is a foundation for sobriety and the cornerstone for taking responsibility for your emotional well-being.

Briefly stated, neither the past nor other people force us to be miserable. Every day is an opportunity to find beauty, goodness, and positive experiences both in the present and in memory. Our happiness, and therefore our success in recovery, is related to the practice of gratitude. Like forgiveness, gratitude is not just an emotion—it is a choice. A pithy quotation attributed to Abraham Lincoln declares that most folks are about as happy as they make up their minds to be. We will show you that your happiness is impacted by what you choose to pay attention to and how often you direct your attention to what is good instead of what has hurt you.

Our nervous systems are wired to focus on danger. Our brains attend to the negative more easily than the positive. We have a negativity bias that remembers painful experiences more than positive ones. These qualities can be helpful for survival, but not for happiness. When we are full of blame for others and the past, we reinforce that negativity bias.

Learning Gratitude

We have the capacity to teach our minds and attention to see more of the good that is in our lives. This is the teaching and goal of this chapter. Forgiveness emerges from a more balanced and accurate memory and experience of our lives. Forgiveness in part is a natural consequence to our noticing and appreciating a more beautiful world.

I (Lyndon) found this to be true personally. After my life fell apart following 9/11, I spent the better part of the decade dwelling on how horrible my life was. When Fred spoke to me about the importance of gratitude, my first emotional response was that he did not have a clue about what I was going through, about my level of misery. You may be thinking similar things as we begin this chapter on gratitude.

We would like to challenge this negative thinking with two questions for you to reflect on: What your life would be like if you spent less time dwelling on your suffering? What would it be like to have more time to embrace gratitude and appreciation for what is positive and good?

Let's begin learning gratitude now. On the left, list three things that are painful about your life right now. For example, maybe you are struggling with the fact that you cannot participate in lifting a glass of champagne at your daughter's wedding. Maybe you feel like you have to remain guarded against relapse, and you miss being able to just let go with and enjoy the joviality of the moment.

On the right, write down three things you are grateful for. Maybe you can find gratitude in lifting a glass of grape juice in celebration because your experiences have taught you just how precious life is. You are not able share a champagne toast with your family at the wedding, but you can share in something equally precious—a dance with the bride!

How My Life Is Challenged	How My life Is Abundant

Since we already tend to dwell on our challenges, let's spend some time to deepen our experience of our positive experiences, which we sometimes refer to in a secular way as blessings. Is there a song that describes how you feel with the positive side? Or is there a color or painting that comes to mind? Write these down here.

_____

_____

_____

How do you feel in your body when contemplating a blessing? In your mind?

_____

_____

_____

In your life right now, how much attention and time do you give to your challenges versus your good tidings?

_____

_____

What might help you give less attention to your challenges and more attention to your blessings? For example: What relationships work for you? What do you like about your home? What beauty is in your natural environment? Do you appreciate your food, clothing, and shelter?

_____

_____

_____

Remember, there is nothing wrong with being upset that you have been passed over for a deserved promotion, or a boss has mistreated you, or a spouse has cheated on you, or you have been stricken with an illness. But after a time to grieve, if you focus *only* on these losses, you will not be as happy as you can be. And every day you focus on your grievance is a day that you are working *against your recovery*. It is that simple. The result of this choice determines whether you will continue to be a victim in a crappy victim-based story, or the hero of a strong and noble story.

Challenges and Gratitude: Which Wolf Will You Feed?

There are many versions of this well-known parable about a grandfather teaching his grandson about life. We share one here:

"A fight is going on inside me," he said to the boy. It is a terrible fight, and it is between two wolves. One is evil—he is anger, envy, sorrow, regret, greed, arrogance, self-pity, guilt, resentment, inferiority, lies, false pride, superiority, and ego."

He continued, "The other is good—he is joy, peace, love, hope, serenity, humility, kindness, benevolence, empathy, generosity, truth, compassion, and faith. The same fight is going on inside you—and inside every other person, too."

The grandson thought about it for a minute and then asked, "Which wolf will win?"

The grandfather replied, "The one you feed."

Your attention is the most elemental part of your life that is under your control. There is a fundamental question that informs your well-being and your sobriety: what will you give your attention to? The science is clear: what we pay attention to grows in power. *Neuroplasticity*, the brain's ability to reorganize, to change, and to grow new neural networks, reinforces what we focus on. Want to continue to be miserable? Focus primarily on how bad your life is. Want to be happier? Focus more of your attention on how abundant your life is. But how?

The simplest choice of all is to see the glass as half full rather than half empty. This can be challenging because most of us are not aware of this simple choice. Do I look for my blessings, abundances and love, or do I pay attention to what is wrong or what has hurt me?

Most of the time, there are two possible paths to take after something happens to us that we did not want to have happen.

The Blame Path: You can blame another person, or life, for making you feel bad. Looking for someone to blame is the easiest thing to do. It is a natural response. Casting blame on someone else allows you to feel justified in feeling upset. Blame says that another person or the past controls your mind in the present; for example, "My terrible parents (or my awful ex or boss) are the reasons I see the world through dark glasses. They are the reason I am unable to find the beauty in life or see the abundance I have." What a helpless position this is. The good news is that nothing in the past forces us to miss the good and abundant in our lives now.

The Personal Positivity Path: You can take responsibility for how you feel and get on with your life. This is not to ignore difficulty; it is to keep difficulty in balance. As we have said before, every one of us will get a no from life—and what we do with that no is on us. Whatever has occurred in your past, you can choose to see goodness and beauty and appreciate the people in your present life. And the sooner you realize this, the happier you will be. This is the true beginning of taking back your power from those who have hurt you.

The Research on Gratitude

Regularly expressing gratitude literally changes the molecular structure of the brain. It keeps gray matter functioning well, thereby making us healthier and happier. In 2008, scientists first used functional magnetic resonance imaging (fMRI) to study gratitude. In this study the researchers measured brain activity of participants experiencing different emotions and found that gratitude causes synchronized activation in multiple brain regions and lights up parts of the brain's reward pathways and the hypothalamus. In short, gratitude can boost the neurotransmitter serotonin and activate the brain stem to produce dopamine (Moran 2013).

Gratitude is a clearly a good thing for us to embrace and develop, but it does not come so easily. Robert Emmons (2018) observes: "Because it is a virtue, gratitude, at least initially, requires mental discipline. Virtues do not come easily, and in some sense, we need them as they function as a counterpart to our natural tendencies. This is the paradox of gratitude: although the evidence is clear that cultivating gratitude in our life and in our attitude to life allows us to flourish, it can be difficult to accomplish. Developing and sustaining a grateful outlook on life is easier said than done because the choice for gratitude rarely comes without some real effort."

So how do you change your focus and stop feeding the wrong wolf? The first step is to really think about what holds you back. It is a good idea to take the time to consider why your attention is pulled toward your struggles.

Here are a few questions to ponder.

Do you appreciate the people closest to you? How often do you think about them? What stops you from appreciating these people?

_____

_____

_____

_____

Do you get joy from nature and all its beauty? If not, what stops you? What could you do to give more of your attention to natural wonders?

_____

_____

_____

_____

Your ability to think, live, and interact with other people is remarkable. Do you marvel at your own capacity? What stops you from connecting to all that you have to offer?

_____

_____

_____

_____

Using the observation attributed to Abraham Lincoln, that people are as happy as they make up their minds to be, ask yourself, *On a scale of 1 to 10, how happy do I realistically want to be?*

1   2   3   4   5   6   7   8   9   10

Why did you choose the number you selected?

_____

_____

_____

How can more attention to the good and less blame help you envision greater happiness?

_____

_____

_____

_____

Are You Too Loyal to Your Suffering?

One of the reasons we choose to be less happy is because we sometimes can be loyal to our suffering. In other words, if I choose not to be offended by what happened (forgiving), that somehow means that what happened does not matter. It is easy to slip into feeling like you are holding on to your suffering to protect it or to make sure it continues to matter. But what is that costing you? Can you protect its meaning without using the negative to justify missing the beauty of today? Can you remember the pain without it ruining your day, and can you be loyal to your happiness more than your suffering?

There is only so much room in your mind, and you get to decide what fills it. When you take responsibility for how you feel and are open to forgiveness, you let go of the hurt filling your mental space. You make room to appreciate your children, your family, nature, the loveliness of a rainy day, or your own capacity for happiness.

Even more importantly, a lack of gratitude predisposes us to create more grievances. Life is often difficult, and we need gratitude to remember that both positive and negative experiences exist. If we can see the good along the way, we are more likely to let go of resentment after appropriate grieving. When we have been mistreated, unbeknownst to us, we are determining if our lives have been rich enough to be gracious about life and not react with too much suffering or bitterness. The person who has practiced gratitude and appreciation will always have a leg up on coping with whatever comes down the pike.

Here is our adaptation of a well-known reminder to notice the abundance that we often take for granted and to be grateful.

- If you woke up this morning with running water, you are better off than 2.2 billion people in the world, one third of the world's population (World Health Organization).

- If your sanitary needs are met, you are better off than 3.6 billion people—36 percent of the world's population (UN).

- If you have enough food to eat, you are better off than 828 million people in the world (UN).

- If you have a safe place to sleep, you are better off than 150 million people in the world (World Economic Forum).

- If you can read this book, you are better off than 773 million adults globally who cannot read (Action Education).

We have so much to be grateful for!

What do you think of these facts? Do they inspire you in any way?

_____

_____

_____

_____

_____

Gratitude Practices

There is usually something we can be grateful for—even in cases of extreme suffering, as was experienced by those held in the Nazi concentration camps. Holocaust survivor Victor Frankl was able to focus on the smallest experiences of gratitude: a sunset, or a memory. In his spellbinding 1959 memoir, *Man's Search for Meaning*, he writes that the fellow prisoners who found things to be grateful for are the ones least likely to lose hope or give in to despair. Each morning Frankl cherished the love he shared with his wife and had a virtual conversation with her, without knowing whether she was alive or not. Later it was discovered that she had not survived the camp. But her love, whether or not she was alive, sustained him and inspired him to fight to survive.

These practices are simple ways to cultivate gratitude in your everyday life.

Gratitude Journals

Research shows that people who wrote in a gratitude journal weekly for ten weeks or daily for two weeks experienced more gratitude, positive moods, and optimism about the future, as well as better sleep, compared to those who journaled about hassles or their daily life (Emmons and McCullough 2003).

Gratitude Questions

Name three things you do on a daily basis that are personally rewarding.

_____

_____

_____

Name three abundances, such as running water, that you regularly have and do not take time to appreciate.

_____

_____

_____

List three specific ways that people have been kind to you this week.

_____

_____

_____

Describe three ways that people have helped you in your career.

_____

_____

_____

What are three physical abilities you are thankful for?

_____

_____

_____

Pick one item you wrote down above and dive deeper. Describe the event or gift as if you were sharing it with your good friend.

_____

_____

_____

_____

_____

Now in your mind and heart, say, think, and feel thanks for the above.

How did this exercise make you feel?

_____

_____

_____

What are you learning about yourself and gratitude?

_____

_____

_____

_____

_____

Breath of Thanks

Here is a simple gratitude exercise for daily practice.

Two or three times each day, consciously slow down and bring your attention to your breathing.

Relax and observe that your breath flows in and out without your having to do anything.

Put your attention on your stomach, and as you inhale, allow the air to gently push your belly out. As you exhale, allow the air to gently contract your belly. Continue breathing this way for about three to five breaths.

For each of the next handful of breaths, silently say "thank you" as you inhale and exhale. This is to remind us of the simplest of gifts and how lucky we are to be alive. We can create a stronger response when we center our experience of gratitude in the area around our heart.

After these breaths of thanks, return to gentle slow breathing for another one to two breaths.

Then gently resume your regular activity.

How did exercise feel to you?

_____

_____

_____

Were you surprised by anything? If so, what?

_____

_____

_____

On a scale of 1 to 10, how likely are you to adopt this exercise as a strategy for increasing gratitude and happiness and strengthening your journey in recovery?

1   2   3   4   5   6   7   8   9   10

What about this exercise felt helpful?

_____

_____

_____

_____

How could you incorporate it into your daily life?

_____

_____

_____

_____

_____

Daily Reminders

Here are some gratitude reminders for your daily practice:

Thank a loved one for all they do for you.

Call a friend and tell them you appreciate them.

Donate to a charity out of gratitude for what you have.

Thank a teacher for what they do for your children or community.

Say thanks for your meal.

Write a letter of gratitude to someone who has meant a lot to you.

Meditate for five minutes on a beautiful scene from nature.

Practice a gratitude meditation before bed.

Share a grateful thought at dinner with a friend.

Do the Breath of Thanks exercise.

Decide to give up complaining for a day—and honor your decision.

Believe us when we say that gratitude is good for you: Gratitude is simple to practice, and it only takes a few minutes a day to practice or keep a written record or a journal.

Let's finish this chapter by looking at how Jerry used gratitude to help himself in his recovery.

Jerry's Story

Jerry has faced many challenges in life, and now he has is dealing with possibly life-threatening heart disease. After the initial shock, confusion, and grief that his diagnosis brought, Jerry is ready for what comes. He can do that now because ten years ago, with the help of his family and friends, Jerry got sober. He had a few relapses, but he has sustained his recovery solidly for the last eight years.

His secret is that he became a grateful person. The burning resentments against his parents and his boss that proved to be jet fuel for his drinking were replaced by his gratitude for all the things he previously took for granted. At rock bottom, Jerry had been forcefully denied a transfer to another department that would have made a big impact on his career—and was he pissed off!

After being angry for a while, Jerry woke up one morning and caught a glimpse of the blessedness of his life—his morning coffee; evenings dancing with his wife, Natalie; and hikes in nature with his daughter, Julie. Natalie told Jerry about a show she had seen on TV, about keeping a gratitude journal. She challenged him to join her in this practice and so he gave it a try. Every day they would each write down five things they were grateful for and then share them over dinner.

Little by little, the resentments that led Jerry to self-pity and alcohol were replaced by his new focus on the beauty and blessings of his life. Jerry even came to see the positive of not being transferred: he now had a lot more free time than he would have had.

Concluding Thoughts

With a balanced perspective, human connection, and hope, Jerry was ready to face his medical challenge, which was far from trivial. You, too, can face your challenges and transition from negative and painful thoughts to more positive thoughts of gratitude, kindness, beauty, and love.

Write about any sections that remain a challenge for you.

_____

_____

_____

_____

_____

_____

_____

_____

_____

Write down three key takeaways that stand out for you in this chapter.

1. _____

2. _____

3. _____

CHAPTER 6

Helpful Tools: Change the Channel and PERT

The process of moving your attention from the negative to more positive experiences and emotions is vital for your healing and recovery. The important thing is to consciously make the effort to add positivity and reduce negativity. When you bring more positive experiences into your life, your hurt will diminish in importance. But how do you focus on the good? How do you let go of the hurt? This chapter will give you exercises to help you move along on the process of changing your thinking and finding the gratitude you need to support your recovery.

Change the Channel

Change the Channel is an important tool for learning forgiveness. To begin, imagine that your mind is a TV screen. What you think about is the channel you are watching. There are many channels to choose from, and often you do not even realize what channel you are watching until you begin to think about it.

Now with an imaginary remote control, flip through some of the channels. You might spend a few minutes on Gratitude or Life Is Good. You may be in the mood for a love story. If so, with your remote, flip to the channel Love. Or maybe you love to fish. If so, have a look at the channel Big Blue Ocean.

Our teaching here is that you have agency and choice as to what you watch. In many ways, your grievance is just being stuck on the Grievance channel. Some of us can watch endless reruns of *My Partner Harasses Me All the Time*, or *I Had Rotten Parents—No Wonder I Use*. For others, there are endless episodes of the shows *I've Already Screwed Up So Nothing I Can Do Matters So I Will Have a Drink* and *My Children Hate Me So Life Sucks*. Another favorite of some struggling with addictions is the If Only channel: if only I had done that, if only I had not done this. And then there is the longest running series for alcoholics—*Poor Me, Poor Me, Pour Me a Drink*. And for people actively misusing substances, there is the *How I (Thought I) Fooled My Family* show, and finally—the perennial favorite—*How to Stop at Two Drinks*.

If you were to name the mental channels you often watch, what would you call them?

_____

_____

_____

What do you enjoy about these programs? What keeps you watching?

_____

_____

_____

_____

_____

What are some limitations of your current viewing choices?

_____

_____

What are some of life's good things you cannot see because you keep coming back to the same channels?

_____

_____

We want you to take charge of your remote control, so that you can regularly tune in to the nicer things, such as gratitude, beauty, love, and forgiveness. The world is full of things to appreciate and find beautiful. The Forgiveness and Gratitude channels are incredibly helpful for those in recovery—they remind us that even though we have been hurt, we do not have to endlessly replay the hurt. Remember: we have choices. We choose to play the show our minds focus on. Becoming aware of our agency empowers us to take control of where we put our focus. And remember, not to change the channel is to decide to stay watching the same thing over and over.

Channels to Turn To

Focusing on the world's ugliness, your problems, or what is wrong with you or other people creates stress for you. Your stress chemicals activate, and in the short run you feel angry or dissatisfied. Your body is challenged by these feelings. In the long run, you tend to feel tired and exhausted, as your nervous and hormonal systems are overworked. To make it worse, you tend to blame the offender both for what they did and even for the terrible way you feel. Over time this pattern of negativity and blame becomes manifest as both self-pity and bitterness, which increase unforgiveness and unhappiness. This channel is particularly dangerous for those struggling with substance misuse.

This is a hard lesson, so let's say it again: When things go wrong, we tend to blame the offender for how we feel. This is a losing strategy for life and recovery. Remember, we may not be responsible for what has happened to us in life, but we are responsible for our current feelings and responses.

It is only natural to be angry at someone for causing you pain, but if after twenty years you are still blaming that person, something is clearly wrong. Clearly your mind is not giving you good things to focus on.

For those whose internal TVs are stuck on negative images, we suggest that you learn to focus more on the gratitude, love, beauty, and forgiveness. Each of these viewing channels has been practiced and found useful through clinical application and research.

Gratitude Channel

We all have something to be grateful for. Watching this channel helps us appreciate our blessings. This is a very good channel for daily viewing.

As you wake up each morning, give thanks for your breath and the gift of your life, the new beginnings that come with the decision to embrace recovery.

Walk into your nearest grocery story and marvel at the abundance. Practice giving thanks for the enormous varieties of food available for purchase.

What did you notice?

_____

When traveling on the freeway, silently thank each of the drivers who pay attention to safe driving practices.

What did you notice?

_____

If you have a sponsor, say thank you and let them know how much they mean to you.

List three things about your sponsor that you are grateful for.

1. _____

2. _____

3. _____

Beauty Channel

This world is full of beauty. Our lives are truly a miracle. Ugliness exists too. We choose which shows we will watch. We posit that it is better to watch lovely nature shows instead of complaining about the weather.

When stuck in traffic, notice the beauty of the sky or a tree. Notice the beautiful movement of birds or clouds as you pass by.

Find a favorite spot in nature by a river or stream and go watch the water go by.

Remember what that spot looks and feels like. Call up an image of that now and describe it here.

_____

_____

_____

_____

_____

_____

_____

_____

Forgiveness Channel

To get better at something, it helps to have models of success and to practice. AA is predicated on the simple idea of observing successful recovery and getting support from that. To get better at forgiveness, it is helpful to hear how others have done it, and how it has helped them move on.

Savor the stories of those who have overcome the challenge of resentment and regret and embraced their path in recovery. What does their story offer for your journey?

_____

_____

Remember a time when you have forgiven. Write about it here to remind yourself you can do it.

_____

_____

_____

_____

Start by forgiving the smallest offenses against you. Practice forgiving for just a minute at a time. What is a simple small offense you can forgive right now?

_____

What is an offense you can forgive for only a minute?

_____

Tell about a time you made a mistake that hurt someone close to you and feel thankful for their forgiveness.

_____

_____

_____

Describe a time when you easily forgave someone you love.

_____

_____

_____

_____

Was the love you felt essential for forgiveness? Tell why or why not.

_____

_____

How could you cultivate more love in your heart?

_____

_____

_____

_____

_____

_____

Love Channel

People who feel loved or love others often are better at forgiving. Our thesis is that the offenses you have experienced can be balanced by attending to the love you have given and have received.

Look for people who are in love and bask at their happiness.

Picture a time in your life when you knew that you were loved by another person. What is it like to feel that love now?

_____

_____

Remember a time in your life when you were loving. Ponder what that felt like and try to feel that love now. What is that like?

_____

_____

Look for memories of kindness done for you by others, such as your parents, siblings, and extended family. If you have children, remember, and cherish their loving embrace when they were young.

What can you do to become a more loving person?

_____

_____

How can you make yourself more able to receive love?

_____

_____

_____

Now that we have discussed the importance of Change the Channel for balancing your negativity and seeing the world more clearly, we want to offer a simple and powerful tool that with regular practice will make a real difference in your life. We call this practice Positive Emotion Refocusing Technique, or PERT. It is a short, guided-meditation practice that stops stressful thoughts, and can help neutralize your grievances.

PERT: Positive Emotion Refocusing Technique

As you now know, personal responsibility for your emotional well-being means looking for the good and beauty in life. We dust off our remote control so we can find what is playing on our beauty, gratitude, love, and forgiveness channels. PERT is a practice of shifting your attention and refocusing on the good in a moment of remembering hurt.

Chapters 5 and 6 offer practices to help us refocus on the positive and prevent times of prolonged pain or upset. PERT builds on these and is designed to help us when a painful experience comes unwanted and too often onto the TV screen in our mind. When we watch a grievance too often, it becomes a habit. And that habit includes the stress chemicals and stinking thinking that go along with it. PERT is designed to calm you down and immediately reclaim your power when you are stressed over a hurt or grievance.

With practice, PERT can counter condition the ability of your unforgiveness to stress you out and pull your mind into deep thoughts of anger and/or self-pity. With PERT you can learn how to maintain peace in any situation, no matter how upsetting. We gain tremendous confidence when we are suddenly faced with a painful situation or memory and can reclaim our positive focus. Practicing PERT helps us stay calm so we can make good decisions. Practicing PERT when faced with a raging boss prevents anger and hurt from overwhelming you. On a crowded freeway, it prevents anger from making the situation worse. Practicing it while anticipating visiting a relative you do not like enables you to decide whether the visit is in your best interest. Practicing it while remembering an alcoholic parent prevents you from falling into rage.

PERT is helpful in any situation where you acutely feel anger, despair, depression, or bitterness. You might practice PERT when you remember how an ex-spouse or a parent mistreated you, or when you find yourself getting upset in an ongoing marital struggle. When you practice PERT and remain calm, you will notice your grievance starts to weaken its hold over you. With practice, PERT takes about fifteen seconds and can be done anytime and anywhere.

No one needs to know you are practicing. You can practice in an argument to stay cool, or while your lover is telling you good-bye. You can practice when you need to be assertive and are worried about the offender's reaction. PERT is the most powerful technique we know to help you remain in control of your emotions. As you practice it, the people who hurt you become less threatening. You slowly take away their power to hurt you and replace it with your increased self-confidence and calm. You'll have a tool to soothe yourself so there is not another day in which to blame your ex because that blame is replaced by a moment of peace to empower you.

How to Practice PERT

When you are feeling the effects of an unresolved grievance or ongoing relationship difficulty, that is the time to practice PERT. We are going to begin with the first three steps. As you get comfortable doing these steps, you'll add a fourth and fifth step to practice the complete exercise.

Step 1: Bring your attention to your lower abdomen as you slowly draw in two or three slow and deep breaths and release them. Generally, it is best to observe your breathing from a point an inch or so below your navel.

Step 2: As you breathe in, allow the air to gently push your belly out. Allow the muscles of your diaphragm to rise, and observe the expansion of your abdomen.

Step 3: As you exhale, gently help your abdomen to push the air out and flatten your belly.

Give it a try right now, remembering to keep your attention on your lower abdomen as you breathe in and out.

Note how you feel before and after PERT and describe any changes you noticed.

_____

_____

_____

_____

Over the next week, practice PERT each time a feeling or memory of hurt comes up. Reflect on your experience and how the practice of PERT helped you.

_____

_____

_____

_____

Describe any softening you notice in how you feel.

_____

_____

_____

_____

Describe any challenges you faced in the practice.

_____

_____

_____

_____

When you can reliably do the first three steps of PERT, you can add step four. These four steps should be practiced each time an old wound rears its ugly head. Practice PERT when you have a memory arise, or you create a new resentment about someone or start talking about how bad the past was. With practice, you will dampen the arousal of your nervous system to the threatening memory and remain able to think about what to do about the situation, or to simply let it go. This will empower your decision making and recovery.

Step 4: On the third slow, full, and deep inhalation, bring to your mind's eye an image of someone you love or a time when you felt deeply loved. Move your attention from your lower abdomen to the area around your heart. As you do this, try to feel the warmth and love that you are seeing in the area around your heart. Allow yourself to feel this warmth as a reflection of your love and care.

Describe how you felt before and after doing all four steps.

_____

_____

_____

_____

_____

When you are familiar with the first four steps, you can add step five. Practice of this step can offer you a perspective on your grievance that is more positive and less stressed, a perspective that emerges from the part of you that is not stressed and not stuck in the grievance.

As you practice step five, you will find that PERT has even more power. Practice the first four steps each time the grievance comes to your mind. You do not have to practice step five every time.

Step 5: With your attention on the area around your heart and the warmth of loving emotion, ask inside of you for advice as to how to deal with the grievance or wounding. Listen carefully for the response, which will be gentler and softer than the bitter voice of your grievance.

What new understandings emerged for you after practicing step 5?

_____

_____

_____

With regular practice of PERT, you will see changes in how you relate to your grievance. Share any changes in your thoughts or feelings here.

_____

_____

_____

Fiona's Story

After her marriage failed, Fiona struggled with her anger toward her ex. Fiona's anger stayed at a steady boil long after her ex-husband left. She had a right to be upset. She felt heartbroken, as he had truly abandoned and mistreated her. Unfortunately, the negative thoughts began to take a toll on her mental, physical, and emotional health. Even after Fiona had healed from her initial heartbreak, she felt that if she let go of her anger, she would somehow be letting her ex off the hook for what he had done. Sharing their children with him made the experience excruciating at times. Fiona's anger and regret fueled her desire to misuse substances, and in this Fiona found some relief.

To find peace and success in recovery, she had to release the anger even though her husband never apologized and continued to be difficult around the children and responsibilities.

PERT, Breath of Thanks, and Change the Channel gave Fiona a second chance on life. She found agency when she changed the channel from My Ex Is Horrible to How Grateful I Am for New Beginnings (aka Thank God My Ex Left). She started to see all that she had taken for granted, such as her children and her loving parents. She connected with a sponsor and by focusing on gratitude and forgiveness her life changed.

Regular PERT practice enabled her to tolerate thinking of her ex so she could make better decisions about their children. Until she learned to forgive, she was constantly entangled in relationship drama that threatened her hard-won sobriety. Fiona saw that what she chose to focus on only grew in power. When her focus was on grievance and drama with her ex, she handicapped the parts of her that were seeking peace. PERT practice gave her a way to calm down rather than create a four-alarm fire every time he was late with the kids. PERT allowed her to talk to him, as difficult as that was.

Most importantly, Fiona started to listen to the voice inside of her that wanted peace and not just anger about her ex. She heard inside that she could make peace with her past and that she had positive alternatives besides rage and revenge.

Simple Affirmations

The practice of gratitude is helped by the use of affirmations. With practice, they help your mind focus on the good that is available when you look for it. You'll find a copy of this list available for download at http://www.newharbinger.com/53974.

- I choose to see the good.

- My mind has many channels of beauty and goodness to watch.

- I have life-changing tools like Change the Channel and PERT to support me in my recovery.

- My cup is half-full.

Concluding Thoughts

By this point you have had the opportunity to experiment with many tools in this book. We explored positive ways to respond to your disappointments and offenses. We offered self-regulation tools to help you calm your nervous system. We offered proactive tools of positivity to help you live a life of greater choice and intentionality. We highlighted that to fully embrace these teachings, you also need to let go of some of the ideas you have accumulated about what forgiveness is and is not. In contrast to that tired adage that forgiveness means "forgive and forget," we have made the case that forgiveness means "forgive and remember differently."

Thinking about this chapter, what are the three most important takeaways for you?

1. _____

2. _____

3. _____

CHAPTER 7

The Tyranny of Unenforceable Rules

In this chapter, we will do a deep dive into the thinking process that underlies your grievances and resentments and show you how to short-circuit that process. Our goal is to train you to pay attention to the thoughts that trigger you, the thoughts that catapult you into reactions of anger, self-pity, blame, and victimhood that are not helpful to you and your recovery. To do so, we are going to look at unenforceable rules. These are expectations or demands we have for something outside our control. Another goal is to help you understand why unenforceable rules are dead ends and how they cause you to create grievances. Then we will offer some simple tools to free your mind.

Two big categories of unenforceable rules are the past and other people. We cannot change the past, and we do not control other people's behaviors or thoughts. When we create demands in our heads about either, we experience a lot of stress in the form of anger or helplessness. We all have desires about how we want things to be, and we often demand that life meet us on our terms. Unfortunately, it just does not work that way, and learning to accept what we cannot control is key to our mental health. Everyone struggles with not getting things to go their way. Everyone suffers when they resist how their life has unfolded. It is normal to suffer and normal to want to ease that suffering.

Here are some examples of unenforceable rules. Some are about our unmeetable expectations for other people, and some are unmeetable expectations for ourselves.

I must have a faithful partner.

My friend is chronically late but must start to show up on time.

My friends must be honest with me.

I have to do well at work.

My life has to be easy.

My boss must be fair (using my standards of fairness).

My partner must come home when I want them to be home.

You must not get in front of me in the express checkout lane at the supermarket with twenty items.

You must stop harping on me for drinking.

Each of these is an example of a demand for something we do not control. Each leads to frustration and/or helplessness as the world or real-life behavior fails to conform to our expectations.

Another type of unenforceable rule has to do with your addiction.

I have to have a drink.

I should not have to follow the rules that everyone else does.

You have to give me a break…I'm just having fun.

I should be able to have two drinks and easily stop.

What unenforceable rules come to mind for you?

_____

_____

_____

_____

_____

_____

Which, if any, of the above examples resonated with you?

_____

_____

_____

If you can think of any additional examples, write them here.

_____

_____

_____

_____

_____

_____

Think of a time when you had an unenforceable rule as a thought. How did it feel when you were experiencing that thought? Did you feel at ease? Frustrated?

_____

_____

If you felt uncomfortable, what was the link between this demand and the mental discomfort you experienced as a result?

_____

_____

_____

Unenforceable rules typically make us uncomfortable in mind and body. We may sweat and become agitated because we are pushing a heavy thought rock up a hill. The question is, why do we so often think of things so that are not helpful? The answer is, we make up these unenforceable rules to feel safer and try to manage our vulnerability and fear. It is our way of trying to control things that are not under our control. It is a strategy we employ to not notice how helpless we can be in a world that does not care if we get a yes or a no.

Life presents us with many people and events we cannot control. We are all vulnerable to these experiences. If we could recognize that our partner decides on their faithfulness, not us, we could choose to be such an excellent partner that only someone crazy would cheat on us. That is hard to implement and requires a lot of work. Easier is to create a rule about faithfulness and put the onus on them. Easier is to make up a demand as if we have control rather than deal with our lack of control and vulnerability.

This is not new wisdom. Remember the Serenity Prayer, whose essence boils down to this? There are two kinds of things: things you can control and things you cannot control. Our unenforceable rules are attempts we make to try and control things we cannot control. We do this to make the world feel safer. These attempts do not only not work but also make us less safe and much more reactive. The rules force us to engage in combat we can never win, arguing that we were right and what happened was wrong.

Important to recovery is the understanding that whenever we are in significant long-term emotional pain, we can rest assured that an unenforceable rule—or two or three—is involved. Unenforceable rules are another way of saying we have unmeetable expectations. In Twelve-Step literature, expectations are future resentments waiting to happen.

We are not saying that there should be no consequence for bad behavior. We are simply acknowledging that shit happens, and demanding that it should not does not help very much. One key understanding for recovery is that when you try to enforce an unenforceable rule, your power and intelligence go down the drain. For example, if your unenforceable rule is that your partner must be faithful and they are not, what can you do? If you believe you control them and you decide how they should behave, you are much more likely to blow an emotional gasket and drown your sorrows in alcohol.

We all have unenforceable rules. They come in three flavors and often coexist with each other.

- We have rules for how we should behave, and unattainable expectations for perfection, success, or love.

- We have rules for how others should behave and how they should treat us. (This will be covered at length in chapter 9 on self-forgiveness.)

- We have rules about what life should demand of us.

Many emotionally fraught situations contain examples of all three aspects of unenforceable rules. For example, someone lies to you. You create a rule that they should not lie. You create a rule that you should not be so stupid as to believe them, and you create a rule that liars should not ever bother you.

What are some of your rules related to your substance abuse or things that really piss you off? Write them down here, and comment on which part of your expectation is unenforceable. See if you can list at least one about yourself, one about another person, and one about life itself.

_____

_____

_____

_____

_____

_____

_____

_____

Again, check in with yourself as to how you feel emotionally and physically when focusing on an unenforceable rule. Describe your feelings.

_____

_____

_____

_____

_____

Ask yourself if the discomfort is worth it. (This is a particularly important question if the event is in the past. And remember that anything not happening right now is in the past.) Write down your thoughts.

_____

_____

_____

_____

_____

_____

_____

We try so hard to get our demands met that we do not see the damage our rules cause ourselves and others. We blame people for breaking our rules. We try to find ways to punish them.

We withhold our love. We do all sorts of things arising from upset and hurt instead of doing the one that might help: looking at whether our rules are enforceable. And if they are unenforceable, learning to change them to more realistic thinking about what we control and do not control.

Unenforceable rules are the underlying mechanism of a grievance. The grievance process begins when we want something and then we make an unenforceable rule about having to have it. When we're angry or depressed we react more to our broken rules than to what has happened. In forgiveness, we learn to let go of our unenforceable rules so we can deal with life and its suffering with skill, not uproar or substances.

Let's reiterate that in every circumstance in which you feel significant emotional pain, you are trying to enforce at least one, and often many, unenforceable rules. We believe that you can transform your unenforceable rules into enforceable rules. And when you do, you will have better judgment, and more creativity and joy in your life. And you will understand what caused the intensity of the grievance and how to escape into forgiveness.

Reggie's Story

Reggie was up for a promotion at work. He wanted it badly and told himself it was owed to him. He confused ten years of service to his company with a guarantee that the promotion was his. Reggie could not control the decision about who was promoted, so he created unenforceable rules: My boss has to agree that I deserve a promotion and Because I want the promotion, it belongs to me.

When he did not get the promotion, Reggie's negative emotional response to the loss caused him enormous pain. He took the no personally and created an unenforceable rule about himself: I should not have to tolerate this difficult experience.

He blamed his failure and depression on his employers and created rigid and inflexible rules about them: My boss caused my depression, which is unfair and My boss had no right to deny me.

These unenforceable rules created the rudiments of a grievance story. Reggie's broken inflexible rules generated anger, which negatively impacted his decision making. He took the perceived wrong done to him out on his employers, family, and himself. He started to pay less attention at work because he believed he would never be rewarded, which was intolerable to him. He felt stuck for years because he never examined whether he was owed the job and therefore was unable to grasp who was responsible for his mental health.

Can you relate? How? In what way have you done the same?

_____

_____

_____

_____

Now list three unenforceable rules you have about a grievance in your life.

1. _____

2. _____

3. _____

Solving the Problem

The way to neutralize the pain of an unenforceable rule is to change your thinking about it. Instead of framing the demand that a chronically late person show up on time as a "should" or a "must," you can reframe the experience by replacing the "should" or "must" with "I prefer that she…" or "I want her to…" Sometimes you can really, really, really want something while still remembering that you cannot demand something that is not up to you without creating suffering when you do not get it. Softening your rules does not make you passive, it helps you become more realistic and thereby more able to deal appropriately with challenging life situations.

It is important to recognize two things. First, we suffer because of our unenforceable rules. That is why when we are suffering is the perfect time to find the cause. It is helpful to make this link and ask ourselves if the unenforceable rule is worth our endlessly suffering. Second, our unenforceable rules are not true. No one must do what we want, no matter how badly we want it. We cannot change the past, no matter how much it might have hurt. Everyone, including us, makes mistakes and sometimes those mistakes have painful consequences. Sometimes people, including us, act badly. Arguing that these truths should not be or are wrong is futile and creates anger and helplessness.

We encourage you to change your unenforceable rules to "I prefer" or "I wish." If in your mind you can say, *I wish people would be honest with me*, then when people are not honest, it is not pleasant, but it is not the end of the world. It is a manageable situation, even if uncomfortable. We are not saying that it is good to lie; the question is, what to do when you are confronted with a lie. Reframing your demands to wishes does not mean you will not have decisions to make. How much do you trust someone who has lied? How much remorse do they need to show before they are forgiven? How much upset is the lie worth in your life?

Two key takeaways are that your emotional distress is caused by unrealistic expectations that make life more difficult because the resultant negativity gets in your way. And when you realize that your expectations play a significant part in your anger or depression, you limit blame and can work on solving the problem, such as deciding how to deal constructively with a lie.

In the previous exercise, we asked you to list three unenforceable rules that are part of a grievance. Let's return to them now and transform them. For every "should" or "ought" (or their equivalent) that you listed, let's rewrite them with "I prefer" or "I wish."

1. _____

2. _____

3. _____

When you can identify your unenforceable rules and untangle them, you feel better. When you acknowledge that there are things over which you have no control and frame your position as "I wish" or "I hope," you do not succumb to feelings of powerlessness and resentment. It helps you realize that there are things you may wish for or hope for, but since you have no power or control over them, and life is giving you a no, you may need to figure out another way to get what you want. Specifically, when you obsess over the past and how you or someone else should have behaved differently, you are making it much more difficult to take constructive action. And if you are not careful, you will begin to see yourself as a helpless victim.

How to Unwind Unenforceable Rules

By following these six steps, you can unwind your unenforceable rules:

1. Recognize that at this moment you are emotionally upset.

2. Remind yourself that your upset stems from your current thinking, where you are still imposing your unenforceable rules.

3. Ask yourself if holding on to your unenforceable rule is worth this current suffering.

4. Ask yourself if the unenforceable rule is true. (The good news is, they are never true.)

5. Convert the unenforceable rule from a demand to a preference.

6. Affirm the appropriate desire so you can see your life realistically and dramatically reduce your emotional suffering.

Now, let's revisit Reggie's dilemma. He did not get the promotion he thought belonged to him. It was reasonable for him to think that after ten years of loyal service to the company, he might be a good candidate for promotion. What was harmful was extending that thought to the idea that the promotion was his to control, and if he did not get it he was wronged.

If you have ever been denied love or a job or health you thought you deserved, you may know how Reggie felt. Use Reggie as a practice example for identifying his rules and finding better alternatives.

Identify two of Reggie's unenforceable rules and write them here.

_____

_____

Are these unenforceable rules true? Explain why or why not.

_____

_____

_____

What impact did his unenforceable rules have on Reggie's well-being?

_____

_____

_____

Create enforceable alternatives to Reggie's unenforceable rules, and write them down.

_____

_____

_____

_____

When he did not get the promotion, Reggie had a right to be disappointed, to grieve. He was struggling to get sober to start with, and this perceived injustice led him back to anesthetize his pain through drugs. Because Reggie was not able to see the dead-end nature of his unenforceable rules, he could not grieve his disappointment, process it, and move on. Reggie created a litany of broken rules in which he was a victim of life. The promotion could have been offered to someone with more years with the company, or who had a particular skill set that was needed in the job. Reggie could not think clearly about it because in his mind the job was his and had been stolen from him.

What are some alternate endings to Reggie's story? Maybe, after a period of grief, acknowledging how hurt he was and that the company made the promotion decision best for them, Reggie could move on. He could remind himself that failure to get a promotion does not make one a failure. Reggie might have doubled down on his commitment to the company, asking to get training in any area in which he was lacking. He could make a commitment to honor himself by deciding to explore a position with a different company. These alternatives become possible only when Reggie is able to reframe his expectations from a rigid expectation to a flexible and realistic "I wanted but did not have to get" position.

Can you think of other responses Reggie might have made? List them here.

_____

_____

_____

_____

Write down one of your own past or present unenforceable rules and explore it. Is it true? Is it worth it?

_____

_____

_____

_____

_____

How did you respond when that unenforceable rule was violated? List details of your actions. Explore the feelings you had and the corresponding thoughts.

_____

_____

_____

_____

Now reframe your thinking by replacing the demand of your unenforceable rule with an "I want" or "I prefer" statement.

_____

_____

_____

_____

_____

How do you feel after doing that?

_____

_____

You may want to practice this exercise a couple of times so that it becomes a habitual thought pattern. *Am I very upset? Yes. Then I have an unenforceable rule. Is it helping me? Nope. Maybe I should change it to a less demanding and entitled way of thinking.*

Simple Affirmations

As mentioned in previous chapters, these positive reminders are good to say to oneself throughout the day, and they can be downloaded at http://www.newharbinger.com/53974.

- *I will practice changing my unenforceable rules into enforceable rules.*

- *I will change my thinking in a positive direction.*

- *I choose to think realistically so I can be at peace.*

- *I accept how my life has unfolded.*

Concluding Thoughts

We have shown you a simple way to gain control of your mind and its effect on your suffering through creating more realistic thinking. Psychologists think of it this way. When difficult things happen, we have a problem to solve: what to do with a bad marriage or a difficult boss or a dishonest business experience. They refer to this as the primary problem or the actual situation at hand. When we have unenforceable rules, we create a secondary problem of significant emotional upset and copious amounts of blame and self-pity. The secondary problem usually stops us from even looking at the primary problem because we must deal with our negative feelings and/or stinking thinking.

Sometimes we use substances to numb the pain of the secondary problem or distract us from it. Too often the secondary problem becomes so bad we cannot deal with the primary problem for years because the secondary problem needs so much attention. When we let go of our rules and grieve the difficulties, we are left with the primary problem. Forgiveness is often the best answer to the primary problem, in particular if it is from the past. Sometimes forgiveness and taking some corrective action is the best course of action. In the next chapter we will explore the last of the major forgiveness tools that help us move ahead toward a constructive future. We call that the positive intention story.

What issues or thoughts arise for you now that might need work?

_____

_____

_____

_____

_____

_____

_____

_____

What are the three most important takeaways for you?

1. _____

2. _____

3. _____

CHAPTER 8

Change the Story, Change Your Life

Forgiveness at its core is a change in story. It means authoring a new story that replaces a tired old grievance. Forgiveness moves the focus from a grievance in the past to a story about your present life or one oriented toward a hopeful future. All the forgiveness tools and practices you have been learning have as their aim helping you tell a better story about your life. When you forgive, your story will still include your painful past, but the pain will not be the full story. Instead of being a roadblock to your happiness the grudge becomes a speed bump in the story you tell. In this chapter, we are going to walk you through rewriting your grievance story as a forgiveness story.

As we begin this chapter, take a few deep breaths, and give thanks for being right here, right now, and for having the privilege of doing this work to strengthen your recovery.

Take a minute and consider the prospect of rewriting your story. How does that make you feel?

_____

_____

_____

What are your goals for this chapter?

_____

_____

What are your goals for your forgiveness journey at this point?

_____

_____

Forgiveness is not a linear process. It does not necessarily follow from A to B to C in a straight line. You may work through several of the steps only to get hung up on another one. That is one of the reasons we offer you a multiplicity of tools. Some will be more useful than others for different people at different times. All the tools are designed to ease you out of complaining about your life and blaming the past for ruining your present.

What concerns, if any, do you have about this next step?

_____

_____

_____

_____

_____

_____

Reflecting on Your Journey to This Point

Let's pause to remember where we have been. As you are making progress, just offer a breath of thanks for undertaking this journey. Compared to where you were when you began this process, on a scale of 1 to 10 (with ten being greatest peace), what is the level of acceptance you feel right now?

1   2   3   4   5   6   7   8   9   10

Write a sentence or two telling why you chose that level.

_____

_____

_____

_____

Take a look at the topics you have worked on so far:

- We started this workbook with what forgiveness is and is not.

- We shared our grievance stories and explained how they are formed.

- We had an honest look at our revenge fantasies associated with our grievances.

- We looked at self-regulation and gratitude.

- We examined our unenforceable rules.

- We reminded ourselves about the importance of not taking things too personally.

Which areas resonated with you most? Which were the most challenging?

_____

_____

_____

_____

_____

Writing Your Forgiveness Story

The ability to face a challenge and rise above it is the action of a hero, and that hero becomes the creator of a positive, rewarding life. The dirty little secret that separates the victim and hero is the creative power of the story you tell yourself and others about what happened. That creative power works toward both suffering or healing, depending on how you cope and if you are able to move ahead and not stay stuck in the past.

Now it is time to go further with forgiveness and let go of the story that has been sapping your will and hopefulness. Letting go may sound vague and nebulous to you. What it means is writing your grievance story in a new way, so it is in tune with a productive life today. Letting go means we add gratitude to our story, and we focus on the present and future, and not the painful past.

Before you begin, let's take another look at your grievance story.

Briefly write your grievance story again. What was the no you got? How painful was it?

_____

_____

_____

_____

_____

_____

Reflect on your grievance story, and ask yourself these questions:

Is someone other than you the central character of your story?

When you tell this story, does it bring up unpleasant feelings and thoughts?

Does your story focus primarily on your pain and what you have lost rather than what you have learned or how you have grown?

If any of these answers are yes, you are still hurting yourself with the story you tell. If at least two are true, you are still living your grievance story, and every time you tell this story you suffer. Too often with grievance stories you are a victim in someone else's narrative. We want you to become the hero and central character of your story.

Now let's look at the elements of a forgiveness story. First, a forgiveness story has no need to place blame. Just because we might have been mistreated, that is *not* a good reason to mistreat ourselves by continuing to tell the grievance story. The key here is that we can be wronged and stay strong emotionally by telling a less blame filled, less demanding, and more accurate story.

Second, the core of a forgiveness story is the positive reason you were in the situation in the first place. The story centers on the positive goal that motivated you and was not fulfilled. Its lack of fulfillment is the grievance, while the positive-intention aspect recounts how you have not given up the pursuit but have learned to deal with life on life's terms, although you may need a different mechanism to get the goal met. Your goal or purpose is your motivation while the wounds become speed bumps that occurred in your quest for what you wanted.

As an example, let's revisit Reggie's story from the previous chapter. Reggie had an unenforceable rule that his ten years of loyal service to his company ensured that he would get a promotion. When he did not get the promotion, Reggie formed a grievance story that blamed his bosses for having rigged the game. His rule being broken meant it was someone else's fault that he did not get what he deserved and also how he felt about it. When he blamed his boss for his unfulfilled demand, Reggie handed over his power and agency and kept it going through a grievance story.

How do we reframe Reggie's grievance story into a forgiveness story? By retelling the story without blame and by transforming Reggie's unenforceable rule into an "I hope" or "I wish" statement. It might look something like this:

"I had ten years' success in my job with excellent performance, and I was committed to climbing the ladder within my company. A promotion came up that I wanted and felt qualified for, but I did not get it. I was angry and disappointed. I wanted desperately to get the promotion, but it did not work out. So I decided to continue doing a good job, and to get any extra training that might make me a stronger candidate next time. I also explored opportunities for advancement with other companies because career advancement is really important to me, and I did not want this promotion issue to keep me stuck. I hope I might be considered for a promotion in the future."

In his forgiveness story, Reggie has no need to blame anyone else for his disappointment. He can lose an opportunity, reassert this desire for a promotion, and recognize how he might need to grow. Sometimes things simply do not work, out and that is part of everyone's life.

Reggie decided to get more training to enhance his skills and to explore options outside his present company. His goal was a work promotion. His goal was to optimize his value and receive recognition and a material reward. The unpleasant rejection in his forgiveness story is not the defining experience as it is in the grievance story, but a spur for him to learn and adapt.

Rewrite Your Story

Now, take a few deep breaths and briefly rewrite your story, *but this time leave out the blame.* Yes, that's right—leave out the blame. No one is at fault. This takes practice to do. No blame, just some facts and what actually happened without making someone else responsible for your happiness and mental health.

_____

_____

_____

_____

_____

_____

_____

_____

Understanding Positive Intention

We call this healthier and more hopeful story the positive intention story. Let's take a closer look at what it means to focus on the positive intention aspect of a story.

Remember a love affair that went south in a way that hurt or disappointed you. Briefly describe the bad ending.

_____

_____

_____

_____

Now think about why you were in the relationship. What did you hope to gain?

_____

_____

What positive reason motivated you to join with that person?

_____

_____

For most people, the positive reason involves some form of connection, love, family, or partnership. That positive intention is what we do not want to lose touch with.

Now briefly write down a story where you acknowledge your positive goal; the most common are for positive relationships, love, safety, accomplishment, money, success, and/or health.

Be sure that your story acknowledges the loss of the relationship that ended badly and insists that loss will not keep you from the long-term goal of creating a good relationship.

_____

_____

_____

_____

Now let's create a positive-intention story for another grievance.

Ask yourself why you were in the situation in the first place. What was your personal positive goal? Make sure to reframe an unenforceable rule from your grievance story as an "I hoped" or "I wished" statement.

_____

_____

_____

What went wrong in this specific painful situation? Be sure not to cast any blame in your response.

_____

_____

_____

What positive actions can you take to get the positive goal that was stymied now met?

_____

_____

_____

What have you learned about yourself or life as a result of dealing with this painful experience?

_____

_____

_____

How can you use what you have learned to go forward in a positive manner?

_____

_____

Juanita's Story

Juanita had a well-paying job as a paralegal at a local law firm. She helped generate a financial cushion for her husband, Jose, and their two children—Juan, who is twelve, and Sofia, who is nine. Juanita had worked hard for the firm for nine years, but each year the stress seemed to increase. She felt that she was unfairly asked to do more work than the male paralegals. The briefs she prepared for the partner she assisted were so thorough that he only had to rubber-stamp his name and turn them in—and he made ten times the salary she did! Because she was good, she was asked to do more, limiting her time with her family. She was pissed.

Juanita made a regular habit of stopping off at Señor Tequila's restaurant on her way home from work. Margarita Mondays became the highlight of her week as she gathered with her new friends to talk about how unfair things were. Unfortunately, one margarita would lead to four, and soon Juanita was not only neglecting the needs of her family but also getting into trouble at work. After many suggestions at work to get it together, Juanita was fired. Initially she did not tell her family.

When Jose found out what happened, he was livid. The children were shocked and hurt. Mom had failed the family. That was when her cousin who worked at a treatment center reached out to her. With her insurance still in effect for another month, Juanita was admitted to the center.

While in treatment, Juanita was introduced to Twelve-Step literature and began her work. She learned that the #1 reason people fall into substance misuse was resentments. With the help of a compassionate counselor, Juanita learned the secret to unwinding resentments: forgiveness. She was taught about the destructive force of a grievance story. She discovered something called unenforceable rules and understood that she had so many unenforceable rules: she must be paid fairly for her work; her family should always appreciate the hard work she was doing on their behalf; Jose should pick up the slack at home; her kids must behave…and so on.

She finished her time in the treatment center, reconnected with her family, and was ready to see what was next for her in life. In letting go of her grievances, Juanita wrote her forgiveness story, which included a lot of learning about her anger and self-pity as well as a commitment to excellence at work and home. She developed a supportive circle of new friends and reconnected with old ones, and this gave her the encouragement she needed to sustain her recovery.

With her family's support (and Jose picking up some slack at home) Juanita got a job at a law firm with a more supportive partner and more equitable pay.

How do you feel about Juanita's story? Write down a few thoughts.

_____

_____

How did Juanita create her experience as a victim? How did she use unenforceable rules?

_____

_____

_____

Briefly rewrite Juanita's story, emphasizing what she has learned and focusing on her positive intention.

_____

_____

_____

_____

_____

Concluding Thoughts

When we rewrite our grievance story into a forgiveness story, we move from being a victim in someone else's narrative and become the hero of our own story. The victim speaks of how he has been mistreated, and the hero asks himself, "What do I want?" or "What have I learned?" The victim is stuck in the past. The hero lives in the present moment with an eye toward the future. The victim is weak; the hero is powerful. The victim uses all manner of grievances and resentments to justify their need to use substances. Instead of blaming, the hero does not give up in pursuit of their life goals.

Victim or hero—what is the difference between these two? Forgiveness is the difference. Forgiveness is a life skill, a daily practice, not one and done. Through forgiveness we allow access to the immense love and beauty around us in spite of the life challenges and unfairness we have faced. When there is a total solar eclipse or the sun has set, we cannot see the sun. But whether we see it or not, the sun is always shining somewhere, and each day it returns. The same is true of the beauty in our lives when the forgiveness of our grievances passes.

Write about any sections that remain a challenge for you.

_____

_____

_____

_____

_____

_____

_____

_____

Write down three key takeaways that stand out for you in this chapter.

1. _____

2. _____

3. _____

CHAPTER 9

Self-Forgiveness and New Beginnings

The ability to forgive oneself is crucial for maintaining sobriety. Even if the person in recovery starts their forgiveness journey angry or resentful toward another person (or even God/life), our resentments often morph into a self-forgiveness issue. Folks in recovery often talk about the mnemonic SHAME: "I should have already mastered everything." It is an unenforceable rule to think that you will never make a mistake, and unenforceable rules make us unhappy. In this chapter we will examine self-forgiveness, explain how to do it, and provide guided practice for you.

Self-forgiveness is not only essential for your recovery but also a gift for everyone else in your life. The self-love created through self-forgiveness manifests in many ways in your relationships with others. Self-forgiveness can be a challenge, especially when our mistakes deeply harm ourselves or others.

A tragic accident happened in Charleston, SC, in May 2023. A woman driving with a blood alcohol level of 0.261 (more than three times the legal limit in SC) ran into a golf cart carrying a bride and groom, plus two others. She was driving sixty-five in a twenty-five-mph zone. The bride was killed instantly; the groom and the others in the vehicle suffered life-threatening injuries. The driver was charged with one count of reckless homicide and three counts of felony DUI (Leatherwood 2023).

Apart from the horrible losses and the drunken excess of the compromised driver, we might ask what kind of life is possible for her now. How can she live know the devastating harm she caused? Nothing will restore the couple to a life together. And so, we ask ourselves, how can she ever forgive herself? If you were in her shoes, what would you do?

Describe the feelings that emerge for you now about some harm you have done because of substance abuse. Were there tragic consequences for anyone beside yourself?

_____

_____

_____

_____

The driver may wallow in remorse, self-hatred, and regret for years to come, as you might also. Unfortunately, at the end of the day, the remorse, regret, self-hatred, and whatever other bad feelings she may have will not help her or anyone else. These negative feelings will not restore the loving couple back to their life and joy. However, pain over bad behavior is helpful as part of grieving, and it is necessary to feel some guilt and remorse before moving on.

That brings us to one of the important insights about the work of self-forgiveness: it is more important to do good than feel bad. The driver in this incident (or anyone else, for that matter) cannot change what happened. We cannot change the past, and no amount of suffering or self-hatred will change anything that happened. But might it be possible for her, with sufficient reflection, amends, or reparations, to chart a new course in her life?

Everyone has turning points in life, and the accident is certainly not one the driver would have asked for. However, even in the face of such a tragedy, there can be a path to self-forgiveness. There is a path available to that driver, and there is a path available for you.

Twelve Steps to Self-Forgiveness

Self-forgiveness is the emotional healing required to go from point A of despair and self-attack to point B of acceptance and peace. We will show you step by step how to do it.

Step 1. Categorize the event.

We all make mistakes—some large, some small. Our need for self-forgiveness usually springs from making a life mistake and unfortunately mistakes are common when in the throes of substance misuse: Here are four categories of offense that can be helped by self-forgiveness.

- You fail at an important life or developmental task, such as bankruptcy or flunking out of school.

- Your wrong or unskillful actions have harmed you and/or someone else.

- You have greatly hurt yourself by patterns of decisions and/or actions, such as misusing substances or regularly taking unnecessary risks.

- You did not do something you knew you should, such as help a suffering family member or failing to put money away for your child's college education.

What is the category of an offense you have committed?

_____

_____

Categorizing the offense begins the forgiveness process. It allows you to break down what you did into a category, get a little distance, and begin the process of healing.

Step 2. Be clear about what you did.

Please identify a mistake you have made that has been troubling you. Was your mistake caused by your addiction? How do you feel about that? Take a few deep breaths, and write down any thoughts and emotions that come up for you now. We suggest picking an event that is giving you some discomfort, but not something that is crippling or giving you extreme distress.

_____

_____

_____

Echoing what you did in step 1, define which category the mistake falls into.

_____

_____

While being gentle with yourself, please clearly articulate the specific wrong you committed and who it may have harmed. You need to know what you are forgiving yourself for.

_____

_____

_____

_____

_____

_____

_____

If you feel comfortable doing so, please share your work in these steps with a friend. Or write a note to someone about it; you can choose whether or not to share it with that person. It is common that we think we are alone and unique in our suffering. Sharing can remind us that *everyone* makes mistakes. Confessing what you have done also prevents you from slipping into denial, suppression, repression, and forgetting.

Step 3. Understand what you want.

You may not necessarily want to reconcile with the person you hurt. Maybe you just want to get rid of the shame, release the blame, and feel calm and whole at your center.

When choosing self-forgiveness, many people say that they want to accept their mistakes, relieve their suffering, and get rid of the shame they feel. They want to release themselves from suffering over their behavior.

A reminder: Remorse over past behavior is not a bad thing. When you feel remorse, you are often seeing your behavior and its consequences clearly. And through remorse, when you are able to make amends, it can bring balance and clarity.

What do you want out of self-forgiveness? Write your reflections here and make sure to refer back to this section whenever you need a reminder.

_____

_____

_____

_____

_____

Step 4. Focus on the present.

Realize that the hurt feelings, guilty thoughts, and the tense muscles you feel whenever you think of your offense is what is actually making you suffer now—not what you did in the past. It is your reaction to it today that is what you are struggling with.

Let's identify how you are experiencing your offense today. What are you thinking and feeling and how are you behaving? How do you feel right now? What are you thinking about the offense? How are you behaving?

_____

_____

_____

_____

Ask yourself: _Are my present responses to the offense helpful? If not, what can I do now to relieve myself of my self-condemnation?_

_____

Step 5. End self-attack.

The key to the practice of self-forgiveness is releasing self-attack—dealing too harshly with ourselves even if we have failed or hurt someone. We create self-attack, and we can stop it. A limited self-attack can be helpful at first to clarify what we did wrong, and then to remind us not to do again. Dwelling on self-attack is often called remorse. You can tell that long-term self-attack is happening if you are experiencing excessive shame and guilt. How do you feel emotionally when that happens? Where do you feel it in your body?

_____

_____

_____

_____

It may help to note the difference between guilt and shame. Someone who is feeling guilt might say, "I did something bad." Someone who is feeling shame might say, "I *am* bad." Which of these do you feel the most when you think about your past offense? What evidence did you use to make the distinction?

_____

_____

_____

_____

While guilt can be a helpful emotion that connects us to our moral compass and helps us make amends when we make mistakes, shame can be a toxic emotion. Shame is linked with addiction, depression, violence, bullying, suicide, and eating disorders, while remorse and guilt are not.

Shame is a basic feeling of inferiority: seeing yourself as a failure or feeling unacceptable to others. Shame has us thinking *I'm not good enough*. Shame emerges from having unenforceable rules about ourselves.

How do you feel about that? Write down any thoughts that come to mind.

_____

_____

_____

_____

_____

_____

Describe any shame you feel.

_____

_____

_____

_____

Self-attack attempts to make things better by criticizing yourself. Guilt can be a useful emotion for developing a corrective behavior, but combined with shame in the experience of self-attack, it simply leaves you feeling bad about yourself.

What are some thoughts or emotions you often have when you've been self-attacking for a long time?

_____

_____

_____

_____

What could you do to give up self-attack and see yourself more realistically?

_____

_____

Step 6. Own your unrealistic expectations.

Most of us have a set of unconscious rules hovering in the back of our minds about how we expect ourselves to behave. These rules are demands or expectations that you do not control; for example, past behavior that you now think should have been different, or the belief that you must be a certain way. But those rules, many of which we picked up in childhood, are not always realistic. Remember our section on unenforceable rules? It is an unenforceable rule to think that you have to be perfect. Your unenforceable rules about yourself are a major reason that you suffer.

What are one or two unenforceable rules you have about the mistake(s) you made?

_____

_____

_____

Now ask yourself if each rule is true. What do you get as a response?

_____

_____

Please craft a more realistic expectation, such as "I wish I had behaved differently but I didn't." Or "I choose to stop using" rather than "I have to stop using."

_____

_____

Remember, it is the unrealistic aspect of your rules that is the significant part of why you struggle to forgive yourself.

Step 7. Hit the stop button.

Replaying what you did over and over again in your head is not going to help you or the person you hurt. It just makes you feel bad and contributes nothing in terms of amends or apologies. So, every time you catch yourself ruminating on your mistakes, take a slow and deep breath into your belly, release it, and immediately shift your attention by looking away; moving your body; stepping away; repeating an affirmation aloud; or visualizing your negative thought floating away in a bubble. With practice you will find this highly effective.

Reflect: When do you tend to replay an event over and over in your head?

_____

_____

What can you do to remind yourself to stop ruminating?

_____

_____

Describe what you will do when you find yourself ruminating.

_____

_____

_____

_____

Step 8. Apologize.

When you cannot forgive yourself because of something you did that harmed someone else, either by omission or commission, you have some work to do. Sometimes all it takes is a sincere apology to make things right. Apologies are most effective if made in person, but if that is not possible, consider writing a letter or an email.

Sincere apologies include four key steps:

1. You admit something you did was wrong.

2. You acknowledge that your wrong caused them pain, and that their pain is legitimate.

3. You apologize for the wrong and the pain it caused.

4. You offer a sincere effort to not do the wrong again.

Practice writing a letter of apology here. (You can decide later if you want to send it.)

_____

_____

_____

_____

_____

_____

_____

_____

_____

_____

Step 9. Make it right.

To make amends, look for a way to be kind to those you have hurt. If you spent half the family's monthly food budget on a bender, make it up to them by turning out the tastiest meals ever cooked on a shoestring budget. Didn't get to your daughter's championship basketball game until the second half because you were having "just one more"? Make it right by volunteering to be next year's assistant coach.

Even if the person you hurt is dead or otherwise absent from your life, you can still make amends by providing kindness to someone else. This is often called "paying it forward." Think you were a bad parent? You cannot go back and change things now, but you can go out of your way to be an outstanding grandparent. Or maybe consider joining a Big Brothers or Big Sisters organization to serve as a mentor and provide some guidance and companionship to someone else's child.

Write down what you can do to make amends.

_____

_____

_____

_____

_____

Remember, it is better to do good rather than feel bad.

Step 10. Practice PERT.

Now that you have honestly categorized the offense, and recognized your need to apologize and make amends, let's do a PERT practice to solidify the self-forgiveness. (For a refresher, look back at Chapter 6).

Take some deep breaths and remember someone you love. Bring that person's image to your mind and feel the resulting goodness in the area around your heart.

Ask yourself: *Is it time to let the bad feelings about myself go?* If your answer is yes, visualize yourself holding the bad feelings in your hand, like a stone, and then letting them go.

Continue deep belly breathing and try to picture the clean conscience that came about from your apology and amends. Bring to mind how much you, like everyone else, deserve to be freed when you have felt remorse, made an apology, stopped the bad behavior, and made amends. You have paid your dues and can let it go.

Now ask your open heart for any other advice it might offer regarding letting go or making something right. Remember, this loving part of you offers you guidance that is without self-blame and negativity and full of acceptance and peace.

Take another deep breath and let's end the PERT practice.

What thoughts came to mind as you practiced PERT for self-forgiveness?

_____

_____

_____

Step 11. Put yourself in perspective.

Remember that you, like everyone else, have good and bad qualities. You are flawed and make mistakes and hurt people. Most self-forgiveness is about your wrong. But along with remorse, apology, and amends, you need to be realistic about your failures. For example, what kind deeds have you done lately, such as helping a friend or family member during a time of need? How have you helped someone with their substance misuse struggles?

List at least three kind or loving things you have done recently.

_____

_____

_____

What are some good qualities you possess, and how do they manifest?

_____

_____

_____

_____

Step 12. Identify your positive intention.

This is the final step of self-forgiveness. Change your story and create one that looks forward, not backward. Put your energy into looking for new ways to achieve your positive goals, rather than replaying your mistakes and failures. What positive goal of yours was delayed by the offense? How can you recommit to that goal? What story can you tell that includes the offense but does not center on it?

Ask yourself, *What was my reason for being in the failed experience in the first place? What was I attempting to do when I screwed up?*

_____

_____

_____

_____

What was your goal, expressed in positive terms?

_____

_____

_____

Think about your response until you have a one- or two-sentence positive intention. Write that intention here.

_____

_____

_____

_____

_____

Summing Up Positive Intention

There is no one perfect way to construct a positive intention. What is critical is how you change your story to center on a positive enduring goal and not on the mistake you made. For example, you got married to have a loving connection with a partner. Maybe you screwed up your marriage big time.

When you remember your positive intention, you take the negative behavior off center stage in your life and put your growth and recovery in its place. Telling your story from your positive intention creates an energetic shift in which doing good is better than feeling bad, and you focus on the positive intention that endures, not the offense that got in the way.

Remember, the positive intention story does not deny the pain and suffering of your mistakes, or imagine a world filled only with beauty and goodness. But it does put the pain into a context that allows you to move forward. Remember, your goal is to do good in the world, not feel bad about the past. No one benefits from your self-attack once you have experienced sufficient remorse to want to make amends and let it go.

Self-forgiveness is the power you feel as you reckon with your failures and mistakes and create a hero's story where you overcome your mistakes or weaknesses. In your hero's story, you talk about how you coped, how you forgave yourself, and how you made amends and moved forward. In that story, you remind yourself that you are a survivor. Promise yourself you will not tell the failure story any longer. In other words, discontinue the self-attack.

To do this, you tell the story from the point of view of your positive intention, not from the mistakes you made. You tell the story looking forward, not in the rear-view mirror.

Can you see that the choice to forgive yourself is a heroic choice? Why or why not?

_____

_____

_____

_____

_____

As you connect to your positive intention, you deserve self-forgiveness. When you talk about your positive intention, take responsibility for what you did, apologize, and make amends, you can now wholeheartedly give yourself a break. The positive intention story allows you to speak about what you did and no longer be burdened by your past.

Have you discovered the truth of this in your life? Write your thoughts here.

_____

_____

_____

_____

_____

_____

One of the most moving and powerful experiences in a Twelve-Step meeting is hearing someone describe how they were powerless in the face of alcohol or other substances. They tell their story not to wallow in the pain and mistakes of their past, but to encourage others by sharing how they got to sobriety and started putting the pieces of their lives back together. Likewise, we encourage you to practice telling your positive intention story first inside your head and then to a handful of trusted people.

Energetic Practices to Deepen Self-Forgiveness

The self-forgiveness energy-based practices in this section have been adapted with permission from the work of my (Fred's) friend and colleague, Joy Crough. Joy has years of bodywork and other energetic healing practices that focus on forgiveness. She is part of the field of energy psychology that we think helpful when it comes to self-forgiveness. Energy psychology seeks to understand the connection between our mind, body, and cellular levels.

This field is based on the premise that there are energies that flow through us that at times can be helpful, and at other times, can be destructive. For example, anger will raise your blood pressure, increase your heart rate, and limit blood flow to other vital parts of the body. This is incredibly useful if, for example, you are hiking across the African savannah and a hungry lion spots you. Or if you are walking down the street in a big city and are threatened in a sexual way. Unfortunately, a remembered offense also creates the energy of anger for no useful purpose.

Adapting Joy's work with energetics allows us to see how these practices work to enable self-forgiveness. Often when facing a challenge (such as trying to refrain from drinking), we find ways for anger to inspire us. Our anger at not being able to drink can create an oppositional energy in our body that, while helpful (because anger is better than drinking), may not be the most effective. Making peace with not being able to drink by accepting your limitations offers a more peaceful strategy that does not wreak havoc with your body's functioning. This kind of acceptance is born of forgiveness: you might say aloud to your body, "I am sorry for putting you in danger with my choices in the past. Please forgive me."

Or you might consider a meditation in which you ask your body for forgiveness. For example, for many in recovery, it is a long-fought battle to attain sobriety. There might be lasting damage done to your body because of your chemical dependencies on alcohol or other drugs. Any long-term engagement with harmful substances is likely to have negative consequences. And many of these consequences might present long-term damage. Clearly, self-forgiveness is crucial.

Sitting alone in a quiet place you might ask your liver (or other body parts) to forgive you for all the ways and times you mistreated yourself. This concept may be new to you, or perhaps even weird, but finding a way to fully accept and forgive in mind and body what has been done will generate peace that will make the years you have left healthier and more productive. I (Fred) have seen these practices in use and found them helpful.

Exercise: Guided Imagery

Find a comfortable place to sit quietly for five to ten minutes.

Take a few deep breaths and let your body relax.

After a few deep breaths, reflect on the following questions, and write down any thoughts that come to mind.

When did you first notice that there was a problem with your use of substances?

_____

_____

What were the signs? A near accident while driving? Disappointment expressed by your spouse or other family members?

_____

_____

What problem in your life led you to alcohol or other substances as an attempted solution?

_____

_____

What was the mental cost of your substance abuse? The physical cost? The financial cost?

_____

_____

_____

Now sincerely apologize for not having the strength to resist craving, and ask your body for forgiveness.

Sincerely apologize for allowing an addiction to develop, and ask your body for forgiveness.

Apologize for the ways in which substances have changed the trajectory of or shortened your life. Sincerely ask your body for forgiveness.

Forgive your body chemistry for not allowing you to partake of substances without consequences.

Finish this exercise by taking a couple of slow and deep breaths and acknowledging the blessing of recovery and the grit to overcome addiction. Give thanks to family and friends who stuck with you, a sponsor who got you into a Twelve-Step program, the fact that you are alive and can enjoy the world. With each inhale, say "Thank you."

Now, return your awareness to the present.

How did it feel to do this exercise?

_____

_____

_____

_____

_____

_____

====== Exercise: Brain–Heart Forgiveness ======

Think of a situation where your heart and your head did not agree and, to your detriment, you chose the wrong direction. Briefly describe the situation.

_____

_____

_____

_____

_____

_____

Using this exact language, say to yourself: *I, the heart, forgive you, the brain, for* [*situation*].

Then say to yourself:

> *I, the brain, am sorry, heart.*

> *Please forgive me.*

> *Thank you for working so well for so long. I send you love.*

Slowly repeat these statements to yourself until it feels like your heart has forgiven your brain.

Now, reverse the process. Using this exact language, say to yourself: *I, the brain, forgive you, the heart, for* [*situation*].

Say to yourself:

> *I, the heart, am sorry, brain.*

> *Please forgive me.*

> *Thank you for working so well for so long.*

> *I send you love.*

Slowly repeat these four statements to yourself until it feels like your brain has forgiven your heart.

Now, visualize your heart and brain working together, in partnership, coming into alignment about the situation in ways that honor the intentions of both.

Return your awareness to the present, take a couple of deep breaths, and allow yourself to be at peace and let go of the situation.

Exercise: Self-Forgiveness

Briefly describe a situation you had contributed to that did not turn out well.

_____

_____

_____

_____

_____

_____

_____

Then say to yourself:

I forgive myself for how I responded to [situation].

Heart, I'm so sorry for my response to [situation].

Brain, I'm so sorry for my response to [situation].

I, the heart, forgive you, [your first name] for how you handled [situation].

I, the brain, forgive you [your first name] for how you responded to [situation].

I, the liver, forgive you [your first name] for the toxicity (foods, beverages, substances) you inflicted upon me in handling [situation].

Repeat to yourself:

I'm so sorry.

Please forgive me.

Thank you for working so well for so long.

I send you love.

Finally, visualize your organs (the heart, brain, and liver) working with each other in harmony and say:

I send love to each of my body parts.

I lovingly let the situation go. It's now in my past.

I fully love and accept myself as I bring forth a healthier me

Return your awareness to the present, take a couple of deep breaths and release the experience of the guided imagery.

Gary's Story

Gary had been a functioning alcoholic for years. Alcohol became his escape from an abusive childhood. His father was cruel to Gary, and the pattern he developed to cope with that remained a part of his strategy as an adult: booze. It was surprising to see the amount of vodka he could consume, yet still be present enough to coach the high school baseball team.

But things were not so great at home. Gary was an absentee husband and father, prone to fits of anger and depression, especially when his team lost. When he sobered up, Gary made hollow promises to his wife and son to quit drinking time and time again. But ultimately, he always refused to get help, each time saying he had things under control. His inability to control his drinking made his wife and son feel as if they were always walking on eggshells. One night, after a painful confrontation in which he struck his son, they left him. They feared for their safety, and, understandably, they had had enough.

Gary was devastated. He missed several practices and, when confronted, got into a shouting match with the school principal. He was fired on the spot. In his exit interview, the HR department recommended a counselor through the employee assistance program. Gary kept the counselor's number but continued his drinking. With alimony, child support and his own expenses, Gary's money soon ran out and his desperation grew. It became a "break glass in case of emergency" moment. Fortunately, he chose neither of the extremes—to take the gun to school, or to turn the gun on himself. Instead, out of desperation he found the counselor's number and called him. That call proved to be pivotal: Gary got into treatment, and now he's fourteen months sober. Working the steps with his sponsor, Gary made a fearless moral inventory of his mistakes, and the list is long. And Gary's guilt and shame are at times debilitating. He was consumed by remorse because of the way he treated his family, and the way he failed in his responsibilities at school.

A friend in his Twelve-Step program recommended a workshop on self-forgiveness and attended it with Gary. In that workshop Gary discovered a life-changing insight into self-forgiveness: it is better to do good than feel bad. Feeling bad, wallowing in his guilt and shame, was serving no one, especially not Gary. Now, Gary is working diligently to make up for his mistakes. He's working hard to be a responsible father and to make amends to his ex. Gary had to feel the weight of his neglect and abuse, to feel the depth of his remorse, before he could move on. Gary's marriage didn't survive, but he remains committed to providing for his ex and for his son. Gary landed a new job as a sales rep for a tech company, and he is slowly paying down his debts.

Concluding Thoughts

As we realign with our positive intentions, we reverse the toxic emotional process of self-attack. When we feel stuck in a story of regret or failure, we cannot help but feel bad about ourselves. This puts our sobriety is in danger. The positive intention brings us back to our goodness, connecting to our amends and letting go and shrinking the self-attack and draining it of its poison. Positive intention frees us from toxic shame in which we are helpless and miserable, while at the same time allows healthy remorse—a prick to your conscience to inspire you to make amends for mistakes made. The bottom line is this: we cannot change the past, but through self-forgiveness we make peace in the present and plan for a brighter future.

Looking back at this chapter, what are the three most important takeaways for you?

1. _____

2. _____

3. _____

CHAPTER 10

Guided Practice: HEAL and Self-HEAL

This is the final chapter of *The Forgive for Good Recovery Workbook*. We have offered you an understanding of forgiveness, as well as many tools to practice forgiving yourself and others. Here we introduce the HEAL method—hope, educate, affirm, and long-term—to forgive offenses you committed and those committed against you. The HEAL method is a powerful technique for healing situations where your experience of hurt goes deep or is of long duration.

HEAL is also a way to integrate much that we have covered in this book in one specific practice. This method is not simply an add-on; it is a powerful way to reinforce and practice forgiveness. It integrates grief and letting-go aspects of forgiving into guided practice and builds upon the PERT practice you read about earlier.

HEAL is intended as a guided imagery practice that enables one not just to think about what has happened, but to go inside the experience. HEAL is intended to be helpful for difficult grievances. One reason why the process is so effective for people in recovery is that these folks often use substances to numb the pain of what has happened, and unfortunately there is no amount of any substance that will make the pain go away. In certain cases, people report the hurt is so profound and so present that it feels like a part of them. The grievance becomes as real as anything else in their life. Often these people have experienced or created cruelties that anyone would find difficult to bear.

HEAL represents an advanced form of PERT, the best quick balm to feelings when you are faced with a reminder of a past hurt. We recommend that you practice PERT for a while and then move on to the HEAL method. The HEAL method is designed to work with a specific hurtful experience, while PERT is for general emotional soothing and refocusing. PERT is a breathing exercise, while HEAL is a longer guided meditation.

Let's use Eric's story as an example to elucidate the use of HEAL.

Eric's Story

Eric was abandoned by his mother at age six. One day she drove him to a Catholic orphanage and asked him to go inside to meet someone. As soon as he entered, she drove off. She could not deal with her life, and her addictions were putting her son's life in danger. After abandoning Eric she was overwhelmed with remorse. She sent word through the staff promising that she would be back for him—another promise she was not able to fulfill.

Eric was devastated. He grew up feeling unloved in the orphanage until he was adopted at age fourteen. His adopted family raised him and put him through college. He graduated and married his college girlfriend. He and his wife had a son. Many things were going well for Eric, but he just could not let go of his feelings of abandonment.

Eric would later reconnect with his mother, and she was deeply apologetic, but Eric was never able to release his pain of abandonment and could not forgive her. Over the years, his relationship with drugs turned into a problem, and his marriage hit the rocks. His son wondered if Eric loved him. Eric had rehearsed his story of abandonment so many times, it became a part of him—and an obstacle to moving on.

How to Use HEAL

HEAL begins with a heart-centered opening and then moves to the specifics: hope, educate, affirm, and long-term. It is important to practice each element in exactly that order. The first couple of practices with HEAL are best done quietly and in a meditative way. After practicing slowly and systematically with a specific grievance, you then can use the HEAL method in the same way you do PERT—quickly and at the moment you need it.

Exercise: Heart-Centered Opening

Begin by sitting in a comfortable position you can maintain for ten minutes.

Gently bring your attention to your breath as it flows in and out. As you inhale, allow the air to gently push your belly out. As you exhale, consciously relax your belly so that it feels soft. Practice this focusing of your attention for about two minutes.

Now bring to your mind either the memory of a time when you had a powerful feeling of love for another person or of a scene in nature that filled you with beauty and tranquility. It is important to isolate the positive experiences and focus on them, letting go of any negatives.

When the image of that experience is clear in your mind, try to reexperience it in the present moment, opening yourself to the associated peaceful and loving feelings. Many people like to imagine that the good feelings are centered in their hearts.

Hold those peaceful feelings for as long as you can. If you find that your attention wanders, return to the unforced rise and fall of your stomach as you breathe.

Briefly describe your experience.

_____

_____

_____

_____

_____

Hope: The H in HEAL stands for hope. The first step in the process is to make a strong statement of hope. This statement presents the specific positive outcome that you desired in a hurtful situation; it is *not* a recapitulation of what went wrong. For example, for Eric, an H statement would not be that he wanted to have a mother who would not abandon him. His effective H statement might be: "I wanted to have a loving and safe relationship with my mother and to know she loved me." Or in the case of someone whose partner left them, an inadequate H statement might be: "I wanted a wife who wouldn't leave me." The stronger H statement would be: "I wanted a deep connection with my partner so that we could grow old together in love."

By making this statement, we are reminding ourselves that we wished or hoped we had gotten something different from how our lives actually unfolded. The statement is a way to remind ourselves of the goal that lies just under the hurt.

In summary:

- The Hope statement should be personal. We are not just wishing for happiness—we want a personal goal to be met. We are not just wishing for love—we want love in a particular relationship. We are not just wishing for world peace—we want to experience peace.

- The Hope statement should be specific, reflecting your particular hope.

- The Hope statement is positive, reflecting what we wanted to occur, not what we did not want.

Write your positive, personal, and specific H statement here.

_____

_____

_____

Educate: The E in HEAL stands for educate. E reminds you about the way things actually work, that there are limits to your control over other people, yourself, and life events. The E is a reminder to accept the way the world operates. Educate means that each specific hope you have exists with the awareness that you may not get what you want. Educate means you are aware that every hope you have has several possible outcomes: it may turn out better, worse, or exactly how you anticipated. You do not know in any specific situation whether you will get what you want. Therefore, you hope, do your best, and await the results.

In HEAL the H is personal and specific; the E is more general and philosophic. With HEAL we educate ourselves to the reality that we are never guaranteed in life that we will get what we want. When we educate ourselves about this fact, we build resilience in life and in recovery. We let go of expectations. Remember that, according to AA practice, expectations are future resentments waiting to happen.

Eric's E statement might go like this: "I wanted my mother to give me security and love, but I did not get what I wanted. I accept that people do not always get what they want, and many parents fail their children."

Take a moment to write down an E statement. For example, "I fully accept that not all relationships work out" or "Not all parents are capable of loving their children."

_____

_____

_____

Next, take a few breaths now and reflect upon your H and E statements. Take them in. Keep breathing slowly and deeply. Resolve to leave your hurtful past behind and move on. When you do this, you are ready to learn and practice the A and L components of the HEAL method.

The H and E statements help us orient our pain and regret and allow us to put them into a healing perspective. H reminds us that there was always something positive we wanted. E reminds us that no matter how positive the goal, we may not get what we want. The focus on our hearts allows us a safe space to do this work of grieving and letting go. The H and E statements are focused on the past. The A and L statements that come next are for the present and future.

Affirm: Your A statement affirms your positive intention. Positive intention reminds us of the life goals that have shifted aside because of our focus on something we did not get. Affirming our positive intention reminds us that we can grow from any hurtful experience. The A statement means: "I am going to affirm my positive goals and I am not going to stop just because something got in my way. I am going to do things to make my positive intention manifest. I am not giving up." Forgiveness is an entree into a mature acceptance of the ups and downs of life, with a resilient commitment to keep on doing the best you can to get your legitimate needs met.

After acknowledging in your E statement that you might not get what you want, your A statement is for you to state aloud for yourself or others that you intend to recommit to reaching the goal you had all along—not the specific aspect of the goal as in Hope, but the larger goal. By proclaiming your A statement, you make a declaration to yourself in the present that you are on board.

Take a few deep breaths now and formulate your A statement.

_____

_____

_____

Long-Term: In this final step in the HEAL process, you offer your commitment to live the life you have chosen as fully as possible, to make a long-term commitment to your well-being. This can be a life-saving step for people in recovery and for people struggling with substance misuse.

The L statement is your commitment to your future health, well-being, and happiness. Just as when you join a Twelve-Step program, there are skills you need to learn to stay sober and to save your life. Long-term is the part of the HEAL process in which you state what you plan to do to keep aligned with your positive intention.

Let's connect your A statement to your L statement by identifying some new skills you may have to practice in achieving your positive intention. Some of the training or supportive services people might benefit from are stress management, nutrition classes, continuing education, public speaking, and individual or family counseling.

Eric's L statement might go something like this: "The two most important loving relationships in my life are my wife and my son. I will set aside a few minutes every morning to engage them in a conversation about how grateful I am for them. I will explore counseling, and I will set aside a few minutes each day to check in with myself."

Take a few slow and deep breaths. When you are ready, write down your L statement, a snapshot of a plan of action for living your best life for yourself and others.

_____

_____

_____

Now think about the HEAL practice as a whole and reflect on what you have experienced and learned.

_____

_____

_____

_____

_____

How to Use Self-HEAL

We just offered you a guided explanation of using HEAL for wounds inflicted by others. Now we will do the same for wounds inflicted by yourself. We call this Self-HEAL. Sometimes a mistake made, a regret, or an episode of bad behavior can consume your life. Some people are experts in self-attack, inflicting pain upon themselves, agonizing and ruminating over past mistakes so much that they can hardly think of anything else. Self-attack can be lethal to your recovery. Let's look at Frank's life to depict the practice of Self-HEAL.

Frank's Story

Frank lived an unhappy life because he could never catch a break with his ex, and he always seemed to come up short. This pattern began when Frank secretly and routinely siphoned off *cash he had inherited from his parents. That money was intended for his daughter's college education; Frank used it to support his gambling habit He was always so close to winning, and he just knew that he was going to make the big payoff next time—or so his gambling addiction told him. His addictions, however, were not limited to gambling. He also was pretty efficient at consuming large quantities of alcohol and other substances. When his wife found out he had blown through all of the inheritance, she threw him out.*

The next day, Frank checked himself into an emergency detox center and declared an intention to clean up his life and to make things right. Unfortunately, even sober and not gambling, Frank just could not shake the feelings of guilt, shame, and regret that consumed him. A friend invited Frank to attend a forgiveness class, where he prepared to complete the class by doing the Self-HEAL guided meditation.

Exercise: Beginning the Self-HEAL Process

1. Begin by sitting in a comfortable position you can maintain for ten minutes.

2. Gently bring your attention to your breath as it flows in and out. As you inhale, allow the air to gently push your belly out. As you exhale, consciously relax your belly so that it feels soft. Practice this focusing of your attention for about two minutes.

3. Then bring to your mind either the memory of an experience with another person when you had a powerful feeling of love or a scene in nature that filled you with beauty and tranquility. It is important to isolate the positive experiences and focus on them, letting go of any negatives.

4. When the image of that experience is clear in your mind, try to reexperience it in the present moment and the associated peaceful and loving feelings. Many people like to imagine that the good feelings are centered in their hearts.

5. Hold those peaceful feelings for as long as you can. If you find that your attention wanders, return to the unforced rise and fall of your stomach as you breathe.

Briefly describe your experience.

_____

_____

_____

_____

Hope: The first step of Self-HEAL is to make a strong statement of hope. This statement represents the specific personal positive outcome that you wanted in the hurtful situation. By making this statement, we are reminding ourselves that we wished or hoped we had gotten something different than how our lives actually unfolded.

The H statement is positive, personal, and specific—what we wanted to occur, not what we did not want. For example, for Frank a strong H statement might be: "I hoped to successfully provide for my partner and my daughter."

Now, take a breath and write your positive, personal, and specific H statement.

_____

_____

_____

Educate: The E in HEAL stands for Educate. In a nutshell, it reminds you that there are limits to your control over yourself or life events. Educate means knowing that every hope you have has several outcomes: it may turn out better, worse, or exactly how you anticipated. You do not know in any specific situation whether or not you will get what you want. Therefore, you hope, do your best, and await the results.

While H gets us in touch with a legitimate desire for a positive outcome, E reminds us that there are always forces that resist our control. Educate means understanding that none of us is perfect and that we all make mistakes. Sometimes, even catastrophic ones.

An E statement for Frank might look like: "I accept that not all good intentions successfully manifest, or many people let themselves down through poor choices" Or, "I realize that addictions can present a significant challenge if one is not careful."

Take a breath and write down your E statement.

_____

_____

_____

Now sit with your H and E statements for a few moments. Take them in and recognize there may be sadness. Keep breathing slowly and deeply. Resolve to leave your hurtful past behind and move on. Remember that for self-forgiveness, it is better for you to do good than feel bad.

Our H and E statements are focused on the past while we live in the present. They help us orient our pain and regret and allow us to put them into a healing perspective. H reminds us that there was always something positive we wanted for ourselves. It is personal and specific. E reminds us that no matter how positive the goal, we may not have behaved optimally, and that self-forgiveness is needed. The E is more impersonal and philosophical and provides a pathway to acceptance.

Here is another example of H and E statements:

H statement: "I hoped I would be a great businessperson, with capacity to handle difficulties or challenges."

E statement: "However, I understand and accept that no one is perfect and that in the fast-paced business world mistakes are common."

When you are comfortable with the H and E statements you are ready to learn and practice the A and L components of the Self-HEAL method.

Affirm: Positive intention reminds us of the life goals that have shifted because of our focus on a failure or personal mistake we made. This is where Frank is. He is having a hard time forgiving himself for squandering his daughter's college tuition. Our positive intention reminds us that we can grow from any hurtful experience, including the ones we cause. The A statement means "I am going to affirm my positive goals and I am not going to stop just because something got in my way. I am not giving up."

One drawback to holding regrets and ruminating over mistakes is that they rob us of our power. When you mull over in your mind past failures and mistakes, you remind yourself of an experience where your actions contributed to your suffering. Affirming your positive intention reconnects you with your underlying goals that will move you forward. When you make a strong positive intention, you motivate yourself. You tell a different story as your true goals emerge.

An A statement for Frank might look something like this: "My positive intention is to affirm that I am a strong and loving father and a financial support for my daughter." Frank cannot change his past, but with courage and commitment he can change the present and create a more positive future for his daughter.

Take a few relaxing breaths and write your A statement.

_____

_____

_____

Long-Term: In this statement, you offer your commitment to live the life you have chosen. To write your L statement, identify the skills you have to practice to achieve your positive intention. Frank's L statement is to attend financial literacy training, and to regularly attend his Twelve-Step groups. The Self-HEAL process of forgiveness is an entree into a mature acceptance of the mistakes and failures we all encounter, with a resilient commitment to keep on doing the best we can to get our important needs met, including those needs to be the person we wish to be.

Write down your L statement.

_____

_____

_____

People regularly attending Twelve-Step groups, earning anniversary medallions year after year are the heroes of long-term commitments. Your faithfulness to these groups and processes gives support and inspiration to live your best life—for yourself and others.

Now think about the Self-HEAL practice as a whole and reflect on what you have experienced and learned.

_____

_____

_____

_____

_____

The HEAL method for self and others is an integrated and powerful forgiveness practice to address deep-seated and longstanding hurts. For people healing from addiction, practicing the HEAL method often is like putting on a coat of armor to protect you from the temptation to misuse substances, or to fall back into unhelpful life patterns.

Greg's Story

After serving two tours in Iraq, when Greg returned home, he couldn't sleep and was constantly haunted by traumatic flashbacks of friends who had been killed. His community wrapped him in their arms, but no one could really break through. Desperate, Greg turned to anything available to numb his pain. He started with booze and ultimately became consumed by crystal meth. His life became a hellscape of addictions. After five long years of constant abuse, his body began showing signs of liver damage, and he experienced blackouts and paranoia. Diagnosed with decompensated cirrhosis, Greg had a life expectancy of seven years or less. When he got his terminal diagnosis, Greg found himself at a crossroads: give in to the hell of his addictions, or change course? With great courage, Greg decided for the latter.

He found a connection at the VA. The newly appointed director of clinical care was himself an Iraq veteran and knew personally some of the demons that haunted Greg. Together, they would speak of the unspeakable, and process some of the pain Greg was feeling. The director encouraged Greg to get sober. Because he had won Greg's trust, Greg decided to do so. Fortunately, a Twelve-Step program affiliated with the VA became a lifesaving community for Greg. He began to see again how precious life is. And even though his time was shorter than he would like because of his bad decisions, he wanted to live whatever time he had left as fully and gratefully as he could. A member of the group shared with Greg the vital importance of forgiveness. Greg attended a workshop on forgiveness offered through the VA, and it made a real difference for him. He saw that he had much need of forgiveness: forgiving his superiors for the moral injury of war, forgiving the Iraqis who had killed his friends, forgiving himself and asking for forgiveness for his own actions in war, and forgiving life for the tragedies he had experienced. Ultimately, and poignantly, Greg had to ask his body for forgiveness for the ways he had abused it through the decisions he made for his addictions.

Finally, Greg was able to exhale, to let go of much of the stress he had carried for so long. And importantly, through forgiveness, he was able to make peace with his prognosis, deciding to make the most out of the time he had left. Greg became an addictions peer counselor at the VA, encouraging other vets in similar circumstances. Greg had decided that if he could make even one person's life better, his efforts would be worth it.

Concluding Thoughts

You now have multiple tools with which to embrace forgiveness. The key is to practice what you have learned and understand that you have the capacity to change both your thinking and how you feel for the better. For both of us—Frederic and Lyndon—the proof of our ability to forgive shines forth when we tell what used to be our grievance stories without getting angry or depressed, without needing anyone to blame for why our lives did not work out in the past. By its telling, the story of forgiveness reveals the peace we have uncovered and embraced.

What are your three most important takeaways from this chapter?

1. _____

2. _____

3. _____

From the entire workbook?

1. _____

2. _____

3. _____

What has been the most gratifying outcome of developing your ability to forgive?

1. _____

2. _____

3. _____

4. _____

5. _____

Acknowledgments

We want to thank Jed Rosen and Loren Toussaint for their profound contributions to the forgiveness work of the Stanford Forgiveness Project. Both have been a pleasure to call colleagues, and their work is both respected and appreciated.

Jed has been an integral part of establishing the clinical effectiveness of forgiveness. He has pioneered the use of forgiveness therapy groups and consulted on forgiveness research on end-of-life care and with folks who suffer from migraine headaches. In addition, he has been a long-standing teaching partner with the Train the Trainer work of the Stanford Forgiveness Project.

Loren has been instrumental in conducting and writing up the research that shows the psychological and physical benefits of forgiveness. He has been a teaching and research leader and partner with our work in Sierra Leone. He has developed questionnaires and other research contributions that support our work with the State of Hawaii. He is a research and writing partner on multiple articles that have been published in academic journals.

We want to thank Joy Crough for her help and generosity in sharing her insightful work on self-forgiveness. We also thank Nick Boeving, PhD, who as a Stanford Forgiveness Project post doc, was helpful in the development of materials and early thinking about this workbook.

In my journey of writing, I (Lyndon Harris) found surprises and challenges to be frequent stops along the way. I would like to thank colleagues, friends, and institutions that have been so supportive in helping navigate these. First, I would like to thank Kristine Nutt, LCSW, LCAS, an addictions counselor who suggested this project to me years before it became manifest. I would like to thank the institutions who were willing to explore this vital work with us: The Carolina Center for Behavioral Health in Greenville, SC, and Faces and Voices of Recovery (FAVOR), also in Greenville, SC. Further, I would like to thank dear friends, the Rev. James Minshew, Jamie Roberson, and John Arnold, PhD, for the parts they played in supporting this work. Finally, I want to thank my wife, Maria Lund, LPC, whose love, encouragement, and clinical insights have been invaluable to this endeavor.

References

Akhtar, S., and J. Barlow. 2018. "Forgiveness Therapy for the Promotion of Mental Well-Being: A Systematic Review and Meta-Analysis." *Trauma, Violence, & Abuse* 19(1): 107–122.

BlueCrest Recovery Center. n.d. "Understanding Why Addiction Makes Us Lie." https://www.bluecrestrc.com/understanding-why-addiction-makes-us-lie.

Byrom, T. 1993. *Dhammapada: The Sayings of the Buddha.* Boston: Shambhala Publications.

Deane, F. P., D. J. Wootton, C. Hsu, and P. J. Kelly. 2012. "Predicting Dropout in the First 3 Months of 12-Step Residential Drug and Alcohol Treatment in an Australian Sample." *Journal of Studies on Alcohol and Drugs* 73(March): 216–225.

Emmons, R. A. 2018. *Gratitude Works! A 21-Day Program for Creating Emotional Prosperity.* San Francisco: Jossey-Bass.

———. 2021. "Gratitude Is Good Medicine: Practicing Gratitude Boosts Emotional and Physical Well-Being," Interview, May 5, UC Davis Medical Center, Davis, CA.

Emmons, R. A., and M. E. McCullough. 2003. "Counting Blessings Versus Burdens: An Experimental Investigation of Gratitude and Subjective Well-Being in Daily Life." *Journal of Personality and Social Psychology* 84(2): 377–389.

Frankl, V. E. 1959. *Man's Search for Meaning.* Boston: Beacon Press.

Gilbert, E. 2006. *Eat, Pray, Love: One Woman's Search for Everything Across Italy, India, and Indonesia.* New York: Penguin Random House.

Glionna, J. M. 2012. "Delayed Revenge in a South Dakota Town." *LA Times,* August 14. https://www.latimes.com/archives/la-xpm-2012-aug-14-la-na-south-dakota-murder-20120815-story.html.

Goldberg, S. B., S. U. Lam, W. B. Britton, and R. J. Davidson. 2022. "Prevalence of Meditation-Related Adverse Effects in a Population-Based Sample in the United States." *Psychotherapy Research* 32(3): 291–305.

Goldberg, S. B., B. Pace, M. Griskaitis, R. Willutzki, N. Skoetz, S. Thoenes, A. E. Zgierska, and S. Rösner. 2021. "Mindfulness-Based Interventions for Substance Use Disorders." *Cochrane Database of Systematic Reviews* 10(10): CD011723.

Goldstein, E. 2010. "Forgiveness Means Giving Up All Hope for a Better Past." *Huffington Post*, June 23. https://www.huffpost.com/entry/forgiveness-means-giving_b_620158.

Hinton, A. R. 2018. *The Sun Does Shine: How I Found Life and Freedom on Death Row*. New York: St. Martin's Press.

Hoffman, N. 2023. *Sweatpants & Coffee: Affirmations for Anxiety Blobs (Like You and Me)*. New York: Media Lab Books.

Kim, H. K., and M. Lee. 2014. "Effectiveness of Forgiveness Therapy on Resilience, Self-Esteem, and Spirituality of Wives of Alcoholics." *Journal of Korean Academic Nursing* 44(3): 237–247.

Krentzman, A. R., K. A. Mannella, A. L. Hassett, N. P. Barnett, J. A. Cranford, K. J. Brower, M. M. Higgins, and P. S. Meyer. 2016. "Feasibility, Acceptability, and Impact of a Web-Based Gratitude Exercise Among Individuals in Outpatient Treatment for Alcohol Use Disorder." *Journal of Positive Psychology* 10(6): 477–488.

Krentzman, A. R., J. R. Webb, J. M. Jester, and J. I. Harris. 2018. "Longitudinal Relationship Between Forgiveness of Self and Forgiveness of Others Among Individuals with Alcohol Use Disorders." *Psychology of Religion and Spirituality* 10(2): 128–137.

LaBelle, O. P., and R. S. Edelstein. 2018. "Gratitude, Insecure Attachment, and Positive Outcomes Among 12-Step Recovery Program Participants." *Addiction Research & Theory* 26(2): 123–132.

Leatherwood, D. 2023. "Authorities Release BAC of Alleged Drunk Driver in Crash That Killed Newlywed." TV Channel 5, WCSC, Charleston, SC, May 11. https://www.live5news.com/2023/05/11/authorities-release-bac-alleged-drunk-driver-crash-that-killed-newlywed.

Lee, Y. R., and R. D. Enright. 2019. "A Meta-Analysis of the Association Between Forgiveness of Others and Physical Health." *Psychology & Health* 34(5): 626–643.

Lifeskills South Florida. 2017. "The Importance of Showing Gratitude in Addiction Recovery." Lifeskills Mental Health Blog, August 30. https://lifeskillssouthflorida.com/mental-health-blog/the-importance-of-showing-gratitude-in-addiction-recovery.

Luskin, F. 2002. *Forgive for Good: A Proven Prescription for Health and Happiness*. New York: HarperCollins.

Magill, M., L. Ray, B. Kiluk, A. Hoadley, M. Bernstein, J. S. Tonigan, and K. Carroll. 2019. "A Meta-Analysis of Cognitive-Behavioral Therapy for Alcohol or Other Drug Use Disorders: Treatment Efficacy by Contrast Condition." *Journal of Consulting and Clinical Psychology* 87(12): 1093.

Miller, T. Q., T. W. Smith, C. W. Turner, M. L. Guijarro, and A. J. Hallet. 1996. "A Meta-Analytic Review of Research on Hostility and Physical Health." *Psychological Bulletin* 119(2): 322–348.

Moran, J. 2013. "Pause, Reflect and Give Thanks: The Power of Gratitude During the Holidays." *Newsroom*, October 29. https://newsroom.ucla.edu/stories/gratitude-249167.

Nowinski, J., S. Baker, and K. Caroll. 1999. *Twelve Step Facilitation Therapy Manual: A Clinical Research Guide for Therapists Treating Individuals with Alcohol Abuse and Dependence.* Washington, DC: US Department of Health and Human Services.

Osterndorf, C. L., R. D. Enright, A. C. Holter, and J. S. Klatt. 2011. "Treating Adult Children of Alcoholics Through Forgiveness Therapy." *Alcoholism Treatment Quarterly* 29(3): 274–292.

Ruiz, D. M. 1997. *The Four Agreements: A Practical Guide to Personal Freedom (A Toltec Wisdom Book).* San Rafael, CA: Amber-Allen Publishing.

Scherer, M., E. L. Worthington Jr., J. N. Hook, and K. L. Campana. 2011. "Forgiveness and the Bottle: Promoting Self-Forgiveness in Individuals Who Abuse Alcohol." *Journal of Addictive Disorders* 30(4): 382–395.

Schucman, H. 2007. *A Course in Miracles.* Mill Valley, CA: Foundation for Inner Peace.

Shannon, M. 2008. *Prayers for Hope and Comfort: Reflections, Meditations, and Inspirations.* Newburyport, MA: Conari Press.

Sherman, J. R. 1982. *Rejection: How to Survive Rejection and Promote Acceptance.* Golden Valley, MN: Pathway Books.

Smedes, L. B. 1996. *Forgive and Forget: Healing the Hurts We Don't Deserve.* New York: HarperCollins.

Strelan, P. 2007. "Who Forgives Others, Themselves, and Situations? The Roles of Narcissism, Guilt, Self-Esteem, and Agreeableness." *Personality and Individual Differences* 42(2): 259–269.

Tangney, J. P., R. S. Miller, L. Flicker, and D. H. Barlow. 1996. "Are Shame, Guilt, and Embarrassment Distinct Emotions?" *Journal of Personality and Social Psychology* 70(6): 1256–1269.

Tennen, H., and G. Affleck. 1990. "Blaming Others for Threatening Events." *Psychological Bulletin* 108(2): 209–232.

Toussaint, L., B. J. Griffin, E. L. Worthington Jr., M. Zoelzer, and F. Luskin. 2020. "Promoting Forgiveness at a Christian College: A Comparison of the REACH Forgiveness and Forgive for Good Methods." *Journal of Psychology and Theology* 48(2).

Tutu, D. 1999. *No Future Without Forgiveness*. New York: Doubleday.

US Office of the Surgeon General. 2016. *Facing Addiction in America: The Surgeon General's Report on Alcohol, Drugs, and Health*. Washington, DC: US Department of Health and Human Services.

Alcoholics Anonymous: The Big Book, 4th ed. rev. 2002. New York: Alcoholics Anonymous World Services.

Walker, A. 2018. *Taking the Arrow Out of the Heart*. New York: Simon and Schuster.

Webb, J. R., and B. R. Jeter. 2015. "Forgiveness and Problematic Substance Use." In *Forgiveness and Health: Scientific Evidence and Theories Relating Forgiveness to Better Health*, edited by L. L. Toussaint, E. L. Worthington Jr., and D. R. Williams. New York: Springer.

Webb, J. R., and R. P. Trautman. 2010. "Forgiveness and Alcohol Use: Applying a Specific Spiritual Principle to Substance Abuse Problems." *Addictive Disorders & Their Treatment* 9(1): 8–17.

Webb, J. R., E. A. R. Robinson, and J. R. Brower. 2011. "Mental Health, Not Social Support, Mediates the Forgiveness–Alcohol Outcome Relationship." *Psychology of Addictive Behaviors* 25(3): 462–473.

Webb, J. R., J. K. Hirsch, and L. Toussaint. 2015. "Forgiveness as a Positive Psychotherapy for Addiction and Suicide: Theory, Research, and Practice." *Spirituality in Clinical Practice* 2(1): 48–60.

Woien, S. L., H. A. H. Ernst, J. A Patock-Peckham, and C. T. Nagoshi. 2003. "Validation of the TOSCA to Measure Shame and Guilt." *Personality and Individual Differences* 35(2): 313–326.

Worthington, E. L. 2006. *The Power of Forgiveness*. Directed by M. Doblmeier. Alexandria, VA: Journey Films.

Worthington, E. L., and M. Scherer. 2004. "Forgiveness Is an Emotion-Focused Coping Strategy That Can Reduce Health Risks and Promote Health Resilience: Theory, Review, and Hypotheses." *Psychology & Health* 19(3): 385–405.

Yelsma, P., N. M. Brown, and J. Elison. 2002. "Shame-Focused Coping Styles and Their Associations with Self-Esteem." *Psychological Reports* 90(3): 1179–1189.

Yogananda, P. 1998. *Autobiography of a Yogi*. Shimla, Himachal Pradesh, India: Yogoda Satsanga Society of India.

Frederic Luskin, PhD, cofounded and currently serves as director of the Stanford University Forgiveness Project. Luskin has been a pre- and postdoctoral fellow in preventive cardiology, and cofounded the Life Works and Wellness Education programs at the Stanford School of Medicine. He is on faculty for the Stanford School of Business Executive Education program, where he teaches mindfulness and positive psychology to business executives from all over the world. He also coaches multiple Stanford sports teams in mindfulness and positive psychology.

Luskin's forgiveness work has been applied and/or researched in universities, veteran's hospitals, churches, corporate sites, and hospitals. He is author of the best-selling books, *Forgive for Good* and *Forgive for Love*, which together have sold more than 225,000 copies. Luskin teaches stress management, emotional intelligence, and happiness skills to corporate clients throughout the US. His work focuses on the research-proven triad of a healthy and happy life: enhancing interpersonal relationships, creating a positive purpose in life, and guided practice in appreciation and other positive emotions.

Lyndon Harris is a former Episcopal priest, whose journey toward forgiveness began in the aftermath of the terrorist attacks on September 11, 2001. Following 9/11, Harris initiated and led for over eight months a service mission for first responders at the former World Trade Center. This mission offered support as the responders endured the hardship of searching for survivors and, ultimately, the remains of the dead. His work has been covered in *The New York Times*, *The Wall Street Journal*, *The Washington Post*, CBS News, NBC News, and others. But after the work was completed, like many first responders, Harris's life fell apart. Forgiveness became the essential tool for reclaiming his life. He is currently working on a book detailing his journey to forgiveness following the tragedy of 9/11.

Harris teaches forgiveness internationally, offering keynotes and workshops around the world. For the past five years, he has been working with Frederic Luskin and other researchers to develop and measure the effectiveness of the secular method of forgiveness for promoting long-term positive resilience in recovery. Harris is a graduate of The School of Theology (MDiv) at the University of the South in Sewanee, TN, and is a fellow of the Episcopal Church Foundation.

Foreword writer **Herb Kaighan** was given the gift of freedom from alcohol on February 21, 1984, and experienced a profound spiritual awakening in 1988. Since then, he has carried the message of recovery through presentations, facilitating workshops, and leading retreats. He is author of *Twelve-Step Guide to Using The Alcoholics Anonymous Big Book*, *Twelve Steps to Spiritual Awakening,* and *Practicing the Here and Now.*

Real change *is* possible

For more than fifty years, New Harbinger has published proven-effective self-help books and pioneering workbooks to help readers of all ages and backgrounds improve mental health and well-being, and achieve lasting personal growth. In addition, our spirituality books offer profound guidance for deepening awareness and cultivating healing, self-discovery, and fulfillment.

Founded by psychologist Matthew McKay and Patrick Fanning, New Harbinger is proud to be an independent, employee-owned company. Our books reflect our core values of integrity, innovation, commitment, sustainability, compassion, and trust. Written by leaders in the field and recommended by therapists worldwide, New Harbinger books are practical, accessible, and provide real tools for real change.

 **newharbinger**publications

MORE BOOKS from
NEW HARBINGER PUBLICATIONS

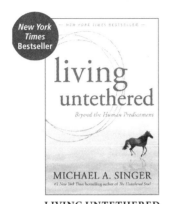

LIVING UNTETHERED

Beyond the Human Predicament

978-1648480935 / US $18.95

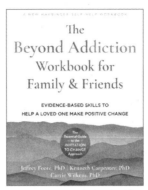

THE BEYOND ADDICTION WORKBOOK FOR FAMILY AND FRIENDS

Evidence-Based Skills to Help a Loved One Make Positive Change

978-1648480188 / US $24.95

HEAL YOUR PAST TO MANIFEST YOUR FUTURE

Trauma-Informed Practices to Release Emotional Blocks and Open to Life's Possibilities

978-1648483042 / US $21.95

REVEAL PRESS
An Imprint of New Harbinger Publications

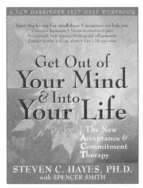

GET OUT OF YOUR MIND AND INTO YOUR LIFE

The New Acceptance and Commitment Therapy

978-1572244252 / US $24.95

THE SELF-COMPASSION DAILY JOURNAL

Let Go of Your Inner Critic and Embrace Who You Are with Acceptance and Commitment Therapy

978-1648482496 / US $18.95

ADULT SURVIVORS OF EMOTIONALLY ABUSIVE PARENTS

How to Heal, Cultivate Emotional Resilience, and Build the Life and Love You Deserve

978-1648482632 / US $18.95

newharbingerpublications
1-800-748-6273 / newharbinger.com

(VISA, MC, AMEX / prices subject to change without notice)
Follow Us ⊙❍Ⓧ▸⦿ⓟin♪ⓢ

Don't miss out on new books from New Harbinger.
Subscribe to our email list at **newharbinger.com/subscribe**

Did you know there are **free tools** you can download for this book?

Free tools are things like **worksheets**, **guided meditation exercises**, and **more** that will help you get the most out of your book.

You can download free tools for this book— whether you bought or borrowed it, in any format, from any source—from the New Harbinger website. All you need is a NewHarbinger.com account. Just use the URL provided in this book to view the free tools that are available for it. Then, click on the "download" button for the free tool you want, and follow the prompts that appear to log in to your NewHarbinger.com account and download the material.

You can also save the free tools for this book to your **Free Tools Library** so you can access them again anytime, just by logging in to your account! Just look for this button on the book's free tools page. ➜ **+ Save this to my free tools library**

If you need help accessing or downloading free tools, visit **newharbinger.com/faq** or contact us at **customerservice@newharbinger.com**.